Rick Tomlinson

Shooting
H₂O

Rick Tomlinson
Shooting H₂O

THOMAS REED PUBLICATIONS
A DIVISION OF THE ABR COMPANY LIMITED

Copyright © Photography Rick Tomlinson © Text Mark Chisnell

Published by
Thomas Reed Publications (a division of The ABR Company Limited)
The Barn, Ford Farm, Bradford Leigh, Bradford on Avon
Wiltshire BA15 2RP, United Kingdom

First published in Great Britain 2000

British Library Cataloguing-in-Publication Data.
A CIP catalogue record for this book is available from the British Library.

Written by Mark Chisnell
Edited by Richenda Todd
Design & Layout by C E Marketing
Printed by Midas Printing Limited

ISBN 0-901281-88-3

Half-Title Page: EF Education *on Leg 1 of the 1997-98 Whitbread Race.*

Title Pages: Mumm 30 Excalibur *at Key West Race Week.*

Above: Rick Tomlinson's first notable marine photograph: the Isle of Man Steam Packet's ship, Lady of Man.

Foreword by Pete Goss MBE

When I first saw Rick Tomlinson's pictures, I had no idea who he was, I only knew that the photographs were an inspiration. I'm sure I was just like thousands of others, waiting for *Yachting World* and *Seahorse* to come out, to see the latest pictures from *Drum* and the Whitbread.

I only put a face to the name several years later, when Rick was commissioned to photograph *Hoffbrau* at the start of the British Steel Challenge. It's impossible not to respect someone who's been down into the Southern Ocean time after time, and brought the most stunning photographs back to prove it. But working with him was a real pleasure too, his amazing pictures don't tell you how pleasant and professional he is in his approach both to people and his work.

The best example of his attitude was in the early days of *Aqua Quorum*. Rick wanted to help, and he did – though we had no money to pay him. On her maiden trip, we sailed the boat round to London in the hope of getting some photos on the way. But we were behind schedule and had to punch into a gale in the Channel. It was too rough to eat, never mind take photos – those kind of experiences always form a bond, and we've been friends ever since.

There's no doubt that he's one of the world's great adventure photographers: down to the Southern Ocean in four Whitbreads, round Cape Horn a few more times with *Pelagic*, to both north and south polar icecaps to photograph the whales and polar bears. I know he'd admit that he's been lucky to see these things and go to these places, but he's brought a special patience and skill to photographing them, to allow us all to share the experiences. When *Team Philips* needed a photographer, I had no hesitation in recommending Rick – we wanted the best. And so I was also delighted when he asked me to write the foreword for this collection of his finest work.

I hope you enjoy this book as much as I have.

Pete Goss MBE

Dedicated to my father Ken Tomlinson, who sadly died in 1984,
just when this story was starting.

Contents

Left: Maxi yachts racing off Newport, RI.

Above: J24 World Championships in Ireland.

Chapter 1
Drum Roll

The Whitbread Round-the-World Race 1985-86

August 1985 – Aboard the sailing yacht *Drum*, during the Fastnet Race.

'I was asleep, but I remember the bang. The way you remember a bang that wakes you up – half real, half a dream. It had been a long day. We'd had a problem with the rudder early that morning. The top bearing had come loose. John Irving and I spent a few hours cramped into the back of the boat, trying to refasten it. We'd finally got it sorted, just in time for me to do my six hours on deck watch. We were fetching with a small headsail, crashing into a decent sea in just under thirty knots of wind. After all that, I just fell into the nearest bunk. The next thing I remember is the bang.

'The boat started to heel, and the first thing that went through my mind was that the mast had gone over the side. But she kept heeling, further and further. Then there was water pouring in through the main hatch, people scrambling towards it. Instinct took over: I swam out through the hatch rather than climbed, but that's all I can remember until I surfaced. And there she was, upside down. With a big piece of sky where the keel should have been. We'd all come up on the seaward side, and I had no idea about time, or place. I grabbed hold of the edge of the deck, and stood on what should've been the top lifeline. We could've been thirty miles offshore. It didn't feel good. At that point, I thought staying inside seemed like the smart move.

'But a couple of the crew – Woody and Phil Holland I think – had been on deck and seen it coming. They had walked all the way round the boat and stayed dry. They tied a couple of harness lines together, and quickly managed to fish everybody out of the water. From the upturned hull, I could see the coast and other racing boats approaching. It was the middle of the afternoon, and we weren't that far offshore; I felt a lot happier. After a quick head count we realised that there were six people still inside the boat. And one of them was Simon Le Bon.

'We managed to confirm that they were all right, and were wondering what the next move was when a helicopter clattered overhead and solved the problem. They told us later that a Coastguard had actually been watching us through binoculars and saw the whole thing happen. The helicopter dropped a diver who escorted everyone out from inside the hull. There was a lot of junk in the water that could've snared people, so he brought them out one at a time. Simon came first. His managers, Paul and Michael Barrow, were on the hull with us. I think it's fair to say that they were relieved to see him. A lifeboat turned up soon after that, and we were all back in Falmouth before we really knew it. It was a bad day, but when you think how much worse it could've been ... Straight after the Fastnet we were headed for a shakedown trip around Iceland. We were lucky.'

The immediate danger had passed, but *Drum*'s participation in the forthcoming Whitbread Round-the-World Race – for which she had been designed and built – was highly uncertain. Rick Tomlinson's childhood dream, two years' work in the making and so near to being realised, was slipping through his fingers.

Rick Tomlinson was born on September 18, 1958, in England, before moving to Port St Mary, Isle of Man, at an early age. Education at the sports-orientated King William's College had meant that, from his early teens, Tomlinson had been able to sail most days of the week – when the weather allowed.

With Tomlinson perched on the spinnaker pole (specially raised upwind) and a video cameraman on the boom, setting up the filming took longer than this headsail change aboard Drum.

His absorption in the sport was total; the particular focus of his attention was the Whitbread. It was the subject of an English exam project. But becoming a Whitbread sailor wasn't something the careers adviser covered – then or now. He had to find his own path.

The first step was winning selection to the crew for a voyage to commemorate a thousand years of continuous government of the Isle of Man. The idea had belonged to Robin Bigland, who was of Norwegian ancestry. He built a Viking ship in Norway and, with his crew, sailed it from Trondheim to the Isle of Man. The trip took three months in 1979, and Tomlinson was twenty-one. They stopped at Shetland, Orkney and the Western Isles as they went.

The journey was uneventful, until they sailed out of Portree, on the Isle of Skye, to do some filming

with a BBC crew. Caught by a powerful gust coming down off the mountains, the flat-bottomed boat capsized. Tomlinson stepped over the gunwale and calmly walked on to the topsides – without even getting his feet wet. It was a technique that wouldn't have been out of place on a Laser. Unfortunately, it took a little more effort to get the Viking ship back upright than it would a Laser. It had to be towed back in, hauled up from the masthead, and then pumped out at low water. The incident didn't stop them completing the voyage.

Nick Keig provided the next opportunity. He built a series of three multi-hulls, which he raced as the *Three Legs of Mann* in the famous middle-distance races of the seventies and early eighties: the Round Britain and the Azores and Back. Tomlinson got involved with the sailing, and then with the building of the third boat, in which Keig planned to race the Observer Single-Handed Transatlantic Race in 1980.

Tomlinson sailed on a trans-Atlantic passage from Newport, Rhode Island, following the multi-hull's charter to a French film company, and made a second crossing from Antigua. It was these voyages, and the media interest in them, that first opened his eyes to a world without regular jobs.

When at home, Tomlinson was working in his father's estate agency. It was a trickle of coincidences that started his interest in photography. Alistair Black and Christian Fevrier came to photograph the trimaran. A friend worked as staff photographer for the local paper. And Nick Keig owned a photo-finishing laboratory. Tomlinson started to take the photos for the estate agency's details, and decided that something better was required than the pictures their Polaroid produced. He bought his first Nikon.

Meanwhile, Keig embarked on a fourth boat, which Tomlinson helped to build in his spare time. When *VSD* was finished, he sailed aboard her during sea trials. On one occasion they were having trouble getting the mainsail down, and Tomlinson went aloft to help free the sail. Having succeeded, he was waiting to be lowered from the hounds (about seventy feet up), when the mast started to lean alarmingly. Unsurprisingly, his immediate reaction was that the boat was capsizing. But sitting quietly with no sails up, in moderate conditions, it was an unlikely explanation. And as Tomlinson gathered momentum, he realised that the mast was falling over. A rigging screw had come undone. He hit the water, more astonished than hurt, and shouted that he was all right to the rest of the crew. Then he realised that the mast was starting to sink. That was when it got frightening. Tomlinson wriggled free of the bosun's chair and swam clear. If he had been in a harness and tied to the halyard, it could easily have been different.

Despite this confidence-sapping experience, Tomlinson was again aboard *VSD* to sail her to Cowes. There he met Jeff Houlgrave, Rob Lipsett and Adrian Thompson, the men behind the *Colt Cars* team, a famous British racing multi-hull of the late seventies and early eighties. It was Lipsett who offered him a job working on the construction of the new *Colt Cars*. This boat was to be a mono-hull – a Maxi boat, so called because she was eighty feet long, the maximum size allowed to race under the International Offshore Rule (IOR). She was planned as an entry for the 1985-86 Whitbread Race, and this was exactly what Tomlinson wanted to be doing. He moved to Plymouth to be a part of it.

And he was, until, in 1983, *Colt Cars* had some changes at boardroom level and withdrew their sponsorship. The boat stayed on the mould on which she had been built. Back in the Isle of Man, Rick went to work for Nick Keig, his sailing ambitions, for the moment, thwarted. It was a full year before an opportunity to escape offered itself. Rob Lipsett called; he was now at Vision Yachts in Cowes. It was all back on. Simon Le Bon – lead singer of Duran Duran and, at that time, just about the best-known rock star in Britain – had bought the half-built, ex-*Colt Cars*. *Drum*, as she became, was moved up to Cowes where work recommenced under Le Bon's skipper, one Skip Novak. The primary structure complete, she was taken to Moody's, on the River Hamble, to be fitted out. Rick moved with her, convincing Lipsett that he knew enough about boat-building to be worth taking. He had not yet secured a place on the crew, but that, too, was slowly falling into place. The boat was launched in the spring of 1985, and did the Round the Island Race and the Channel Race as a warm-up, before entering the Royal Ocean Racing Club's bi-annual classic, the Fastnet.

The failure of the keel put the whole Whitbread project in doubt. But those in charge had the will, and the means. *Drum* was righted and towed back to Moody's. It took more than a week, but finally everyone had committed to getting her ready in time. With only six weeks before the start, it was a frantic schedule. But as

Previous Pages: Tomlinson's original approach to on-board photography is epitomised by his atmospheric low-light images.

Above & Right: Some pictures are made by the light, others by the action of the moment. Tomlinson had to be ready for both.

the boat slowly came back together, so did the opportunities. With Simon Le Bon aboard, his management team thought someone should be taking some photos. With a place on the boat now his, Tomlinson was happy to volunteer. But the precious Nikon had been trashed in the Fastnet. Rick took the waterlogged body up to London and walked into Nikon's offices. Alan Bartlett, a keen windsurfer himself, had heard all about the travails of Simon Le Bon's Whitbread boat. He was happy to be able to help the young photographer.

And so, just before the start, *Drum* sailed back out of Moody's, hoisted a couple of sails to see if they fitted, and then joined the fleet to head for Cape Town. With one camera and about twenty rolls of film, Tomlinson was on his way, in more ways than he might have anticipated. With around twenty crew aboard the eighty-foot boat, there were enough hands to stroll through the work – most of the time. It provided plenty of opportunity to experiment. Tomlinson began to work with the night-time delayed exposures that would quickly become a trademark. When they arrived in Cape Town and processed the film, he was happily surprised at the results. Selecting the best, he sent them to a couple of British sailing magazines, *Yachting World* and *Seahorse*. He was even more surprised to find them published. Astonished to discover the cheques coming through in payment. He was a professional photographer.

For others, more experienced in sailing media, his photos were redefining on-board photography. Encouragement came quickly from then *Yachting World* writer Tim Jeffery, and *Seahorse* editor Jason Holtom. The combination of an artist's aesthetic and a crewman's eye was unique. They put his work in places where it quickly got noticed. It was a beginning. Tomlinson had a reputation and a portfolio. Unfortunately, he still had no idea what he was really doing.

Chapter 2
Buoy Racing

August 1988 – Aboard a press boat, during the Kenwood Cup.

'The press boat had looked pretty small in the harbour, even for just three of us and a driver. Barry Pickthall, the former Times journalist, was one of the others, and the driver was a yacht-club member who had volunteered. The boat didn't feel any bigger out in the Pacific Ocean. There was lots of breeze and a good swell running. But with plenty of sunshine it was ideal for action photography. That first day was shaping up to be everything it was supposed to be – I'd been planning this trip to Hawaii since talking about the Kenwood Cup to other photographers in Sardinia, two years previously.

'The inshore side of the course is always heavily favoured when beating up towards Diamond Head; the yachts have to win the start at the buoy and go straight into the beach. So we set up at the leeward end of the start line for the first race. In the crush – the photo boats all want to be in the same spot – the driver had got us a little too far upwind. It was a fantastic position for getting pictures, but we were in the way of the boats coming off the line. There were quite a few Maxis in the fleet that year. The driver might have panicked a little, seeing them all bearing down on us. Or maybe he just didn't know the boat's characteristics, or made a bad decision. Whatever, instead of moving ahead and motoring out of the way, he went hard astern.

'The effect was spectacular. He just reversed the boat straight under. It filled from behind and flipped over. It was supposed to be unsinkable, and it was. But there weren't any guarantees about which way up it would float. So there I was, swimming around, with the fleet bearing down on us, trying to keep my precious – and only – Nikon camera above my head, while the rest of the press corps were killing themselves laughing.

'The fleet sailed round us easily enough. Then the press boats came in to pick us up, circling like vultures, still giggling, taking photos. They were shooed out of the way by a US Coastguard boat. He dropped a ladder and took us aboard. But by then my camera had gone under, along with everything in the boat. All the gear, trashed on the first day of the regatta. It seemed like a complete disaster at the time. To rub it in, they dropped us at the Coastguard base and we had to walk a couple of miles to find a taxi. The road was black tarmac, and we'd all lost our shoes. We were trailing down the white centre line, the only ground cool enough to walk on. I'd had better days.'

At the end of that first Whitbread Race, Tomlinson wasn't conscious of the risks he would run and the skills he had yet to acquire to make it as a professional photographer. And certainly, even if he had stopped to think about it, coping with the deficiencies of amateur press-boat drivers wouldn't have been on his list of concerns. The Whitbread had fulfilled his childhood dream and, unlike many others before and since, Tomlinson knew exactly what he wanted to do next. He had seen professional yachting photographers at work during the race, and was sure that this was the life for him. The problem was how to make it happen.

Once again, Drum provided the answer. The boat had been chartered by an Irish syndicate, led by Tom Power, who had got Mazda to sponsor her in the Round Ireland Race. Simon Le Bon would be aboard, and Tom knew that pictures taken on the boat during the race would make Mazda's media coverage. Tom had heard about Rick Tomlinson and seen his work – was he interested in the job? Of course. And how much would he charge? Nervously, Tomlinson stabbed at a figure – fifty pounds? Power concealed a smile. We'll pay you five hundred, he said. It was Tomlinson's first-ever commission. Working in the familiar on-board environment, client and photographer were both happy with the results.

John Toon was a New Zealand cinematographer; he had been aboard Drum for one leg of the Whitbread Race. Toon had mentioned Tomlinson's name to Strategic Advertising, a London-based marketing

The America True team train for their America's Cup campaign in the 1D48 at Key West Race Week.

Above: Maybe a hundred boats rounded this mark at the SORC, but the wave pattern only created this image for one of them, Merit Cup.

Right: Classic Solent light – storm clouds and sunshine for the Mumm 36 Group 4.

company that worked for Rolex, and Nautor – builders of the Swan range of luxury yachts. The managing director, Brian Savage, gave Rick his second commission: to photograph a Rolex-sponsored Swan regatta, in the States, in the summer of 1986. This was different. Tomlinson had to work from a press boat rather than on deck. Believing a fast film speed to be necessary to capture the action, Tomlinson chose a 400 ISO film for his Nikon. But it was too fast; the speed of the film resulted in pictures that were too grainy, barely usable. It got worse. Strategic had lent him a large-format camera, normally used for studio work. Tomlinson loaded the film in that back to front, and nothing came out. The experience was a lesson in how much more he had to learn.

But the people at Strategic could see something in the images that had been processed. And Tomlinson got a second chance: he was assigned to shoot the Rolex Swan World Cup in Porto Cervo, Sardinia, that autumn. He had learned from his mistakes. And in Porto Cervo, he met more professional marine photographers – Carlo Borlenghi and Guy Gurney amongst them. They had seen his Whitbread work in the magazines, were interested to meet this new talent, and keen to encourage him. It went well; Rick stayed on for the Sardinia Cup, and then got a ride up to the La Nioulargue in St Tropez. There he sailed on *Drum*, taking photographs when that boat wasn't racing.

Returning from the glamour of the Mediterranean circuit, Tomlinson found himself back in a grey London, with winter coming on. It was late 1986, in Australia the early rounds of the America's Cup trials were under way. The still and television footage of the Twelve Metres racing in the strong winds of Fremantle was stunning. Should he go? But Brian Savage had offered him a job as an account executive, working on the Nautor Swan business. There would be the opportunity for some photography. Mindful of his earlier errors, and recognising that every other marine photographer in the world was headed for Fremantle, Rick elected to stay in London.

It was the right decision. He was able to work on some advertising shoots for Nautor, being flown out to the Caribbean to photograph the Rolex Cup. Tomlinson made invaluable new contacts in the magazine and business world, and got an extensive look at how the media industry worked. It all helped him to find work outside of Strategic's remit. He spent the weekends on the South Coast, staying with friends in Hamble, begging rides to get out and photograph the racing. *Yachting World* and *Seahorse* magazines both continued to encourage him. But all the freelance work started to interfere with his job. And in the summer of 1987 Brian Savage gave him a weekend to decide: stay with us and concentrate on the work, or leave. Tomlinson decided to go out on his own. The next day, the bottom fell out of the stock market.

It was too late to go back. Skip Novak, *Drum*'s skipper and now a close friend, was running a yacht called *Pelagic* chartering down to the Antarctic. His house in Hamble was empty, and Rick offered to rent it from him. From this base, Tomlinson travelled as far as Hawaii, Miami and Auckland, for events as diverse as the Kenwood Cup, the IOR Fifty-Footer Circuit and the launch of the New Zealand America's Cup 'Big Boat'. Closer to home there was the Formula 40 circuit and a whirl of other regattas in Europe. All the work was done 'on-spec' – the photographer travels to the event, finds somewhere to stay, takes the pictures on their own film, with their own cameras, at their own expense. The resulting photographs are sorted and submitted to all the magazines that might publish them. And if no one does, there's no money to pay the overheads, never mind any profit.

But as Tomlinson discovered in Hawaii, there were other risks. Swimming up to his neck (again), this time in the Pacific Ocean, he had plenty of time to ponder on the fact that he had just lost his camera equipment (again), this time on the first day of the biggest regatta of the year. It was insured, but no one was about to postpone the sailing until Rick Tomlinson had replaced his camera. Hawaii isn't the best place to start buying professional photographic equipment – but no photos, no pay. Rick was lucky; Guy Gurney had a spare camera that he was able to lend him for the following day. The day after that, the good people at Nikon had once again come through – a replacement camera was freighted all the way out to Honolulu. And, ultimately, the experience had its benefits. When he finally returned to England and re-equipped, Tomlinson was able to do it with the latest technology – including autofocus cameras. Focusing and framing moving targets, on an open boat in open ocean, is not easy. Any help the technology could provide was gratefully received.

It's an extreme example, but the adventure in Hawaii did highlight the problems of covering a regatta from a press boat. Many of the big events will supply press boats, either free or with a fairly nominal charge. The most senior photographer on board will usually

Patience and being in the right place at the right time for this sequence of a crewman going overboard from America True at the SORC.

be assigned to talk to the driver. In those early days, that meant that Tomlinson benefited from the experience of others, who put the boat in the right place. Now it's Rick who finds himself directing the boat. The drivers are almost always enthusiastic volunteers – anxious to help, but with no real idea of how. By the end of the week, they know the job – just in time for everyone to move on to the next regatta and start with a new driver.

There are several good positions to set up, to anticipate the action. The windward mark is one of them, sitting ahead of the yachts approaching on the starboard tack. The press boat is positioned just to windward of the yacht's track, so that the photographer can see the crew. A lot of the best pictures are of people: expressions, movement, body language. Sometimes crowding from other spectator boats, or the sun shining directly into the lens, makes this position impossible. In which case, the next best place is to windward of the buoy, on the line that the boats will take away from the mark after the rounding.

Light is the other crucial factor: the softer the better, and that means having the sun low in the sky. Of all the windward-mark roundings, the most important is the first, when the boats are closest together. And of all the first windward-mark roundings, the most important is that in the first race, which has better light because it is earlier in the day. In an ideal world, with races laid on for Rick Tomlinson's benefit, the action would start at four in the afternoon and finish around eight, with three reaches and one short beat in each race!

Sleighride at Antigua Race Week.

None of which means that great photos can't be taken from the most improbable places, at the most improbable times – which goes to show how much luck is involved. Tomlinson had been invited over to Dublin to watch the first round of the Irish Admiral's Cup trials. On arrival in Howth, he found a four-metre Rigid Inflatable Boat (RIB) waiting to take him out on the race course. It was blowing hard, very hard, and as soon as they arrived in the starting area it was clear that it would be impossible to work from the RIB. Rick

transferred to the Irish Team Selector's boat, a big motoryacht that was watching individual yacht performances rather than moving around the race track at the beck and call of a photographer.

The starting sequence was running, and Rick had just made it onto the deck as *Jameson Whiskey* sailed past, turning to go down the line. He tracked her through the viewfinder – when a huge gust struck. The leeward runner was tight, the mainsheet didn't ease when it should have, and over she went. With everyone else on the spectator boat gasping, Rick hit the shutter release. The RIB he had just got out of capsized a moment later. They had to pick up the helmsman and tow the boat in. Tomlinson didn't think much more about the photo at the time – or how close he had come to not taking it. But after the picture had been processed, he took it in to *Seahorse* magazine. The editor, Jason Holtom, loved it, and said he'd use it as a double-page spread. But, he commented, it would make a great calendar shot.

At the finish in Auckland, Whitbread racer Toshiba *reverts to inshore race mode, with all the crew on the rail*

La Nioulargue provides opportunities for classic yachts like Astra *to race inshore.*

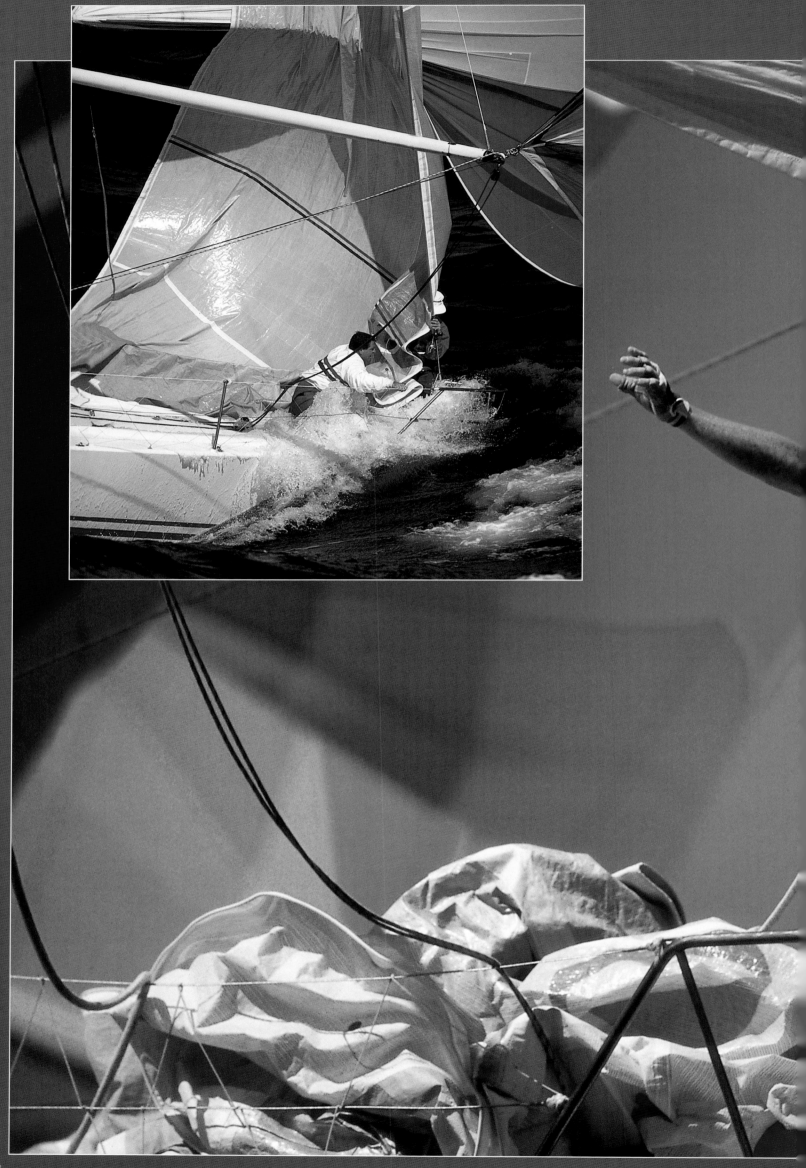

In yachting photography, people are often more important than yachts.

Good racing images usually come from marks and start lines. But another's misfortune – which can happen anytime, anywhere – also provides the well-placed photographer with opportunities. Main Photograph: Corum Rubis in the Solent. Clockwise from top right: Jameson at the Admiral's Cup; Merit Cup at the Whitbread finish in Auckland; Christina Belta at the Nioulargue; Zurich and Relax at the One Ton Cup; Brava at the Admiral's Cup; Maxima at Cowes Week.

The image is the whole frame, making the background as important as the foreground. Other X Boats, and a powerboat wake behind the 18 Foot Skiff, add to the impact, but are deliberately out of focus to isolate the main subject.

Next pages: The sheer number of competitors in the Round Gotland Race will always provide new images for those that can see the different angles.

Above: The 1987 Jameson Whiskey provided the image that started thoughts of a calendar.
Top: At the 1993 Admiral's Cup, the same sponsor was still the source of the photographs.

The Sydney 40 Breeze 2 broaches at the Admiral's Cup.

Left: Large numbers of small one designs equal tightly framed action, 707 Nationals in the Solent.

Below: Strong breeze and the Melges 24 fleet at Key West Race Week, almost guarantee good photographs: this is Wicked Feet.

The Mumm 36, Barlo Plastics, *at the start of the Wolf Rock Race during the Admiral's Cup 1999.*

Chapter 3
The Calendar

March 1988 – The Isle of Man Bank, Port Erin

'The waiting was the worst part. Waiting on my own in the interview room. It had these green plastic imitation-leather chairs and a Formica table. The chairs squeaked when you moved. And there was nothing on the walls at all. It was completely bare. I'd put on my best blazer – actually, my only blazer. And a tie, with grey slacks. Mr Chillcott was the manager. I'd brought along a presentation that Cathie and I had put together on my Amstrad computer. Neatly printed out, just a few sheets in a plastic folder with the photo of Jameson Whiskey *on the cover. The proposal had all the figures, the projected sales and so on. That was for 1989. I think we just reached those sales figures in 1999.*

'By then I really wanted to do the calendar, and this was the last chance. All the publishers we'd tried had turned us down. But those were the days when the bank manager knew the family. My father had always used that bank for his business; Mr Chillcott had known me since I was at school. When I'd explained the idea of the calendar, he was very supportive. Years later, even after he'd retired, whenever I saw him around the town, he would ask me about the calendar.'

It had been Jason Holtom's comment, about the *Jameson Whiskey* image making a good calendar photo, that had put the germ of an idea into Tomlinson's head. He'd sold a lot of photographs to magazines through the summer of 1987 and early 1988, but it was still a very hand-to-mouth affair, relying on the whims of magazine editors, with overheads that were constantly threatening to swamp the income. The calendar could put his youthful business on a more grown-up footing, providing a second use for the best material and a steady sales income. The only yachting calendar widely available in the late eighties was done by Beken. The style of image and the content represented that family's long history and association with Cowes and the Solent. But action race-boat photography had moved on – as the *Jameson Whiskey* shot had demonstrated. There was an opening in the market, and Tomlinson wanted to close it.

At the time, Rick's sister Cathie was a bored housewife looking for something to do. It took no persuading to get her involved in the business and the calendar project. Rick moved back to the Isle of Man and set up the new venture in Cathie's house. That also lowered the overheads, and Cathie could provide a contact point for the business. Just getting messages was difficult for a globetrotting one-man-band, when the answerphone and fax machine were still novelties, in a world before cell phones and email were ubiquitous. Together, they started to research the calendar in the autumn of 1987.

Rick's time at Strategic Advertising had provided some knowledge of the design and print businesses. A designer, who was then doing a lot of work with Tracy Edwards and her Whitbread project, was happy to get involved. The first problem, inevitably, came with the printing. With no track record or credit references, payment would have to be on delivery. That focused them on the second problem – they had no obvious means of selling the calendar. The initial solution was to seek the partnership of several publishers. But no one was interested. And soon they found themselves looking at the print and production costs to see if they could do it themselves. Which is how Rick Tomlinson found himself in Mr Chillcott's interview room, trying to borrow the money to print his calendar. It was a substantial risk. He had started working with his bonus from *Drum* – three thousand pounds, with which Tomlinson had bought a car and a computer. The rest had provided a cash-flow buffer that kept him more or less in credit with the bank. Borrowing the kind of money required to print the calendar was an altogether more speculative kind of business.

It would also alter his work in more subtle, unexpected ways. With almost four years of pictures to choose from, selecting the photographs for the first calendar was the easy part. When the second one came around, all too quickly, there was only a single year of new work to go to for the images. With each passing

*Fisher and Paykel in a sea of light. A calendar image in all but format –
this portrait image wasn't suitable for the landscape format calendar.*

year, the stock became more dated, and more familiar. Shooting enough good photos for the coming year's calendar became a priority. Fortunately, the other aspects got easier, as happy customers built the market by word of mouth. And with the previous calendars in hand, it was a lot easier to sell the next one. But selling the first was an exhausting business. Tomlinson worked his way through his address book; friends, boat-owners, business contacts – everyone got the sales pitch.

The first calendar broke even, no more. But many of the buyers of the first calendar are still customers. It has grown from there, a formula that was quickly established and has remained consistent. The handful of changes have been subtle. The black background became white. The date format was altered from a row along the bottom to a grid. The former looked better, the latter was more practical for the user. But requests to provide boxes that could be written in were resisted on aesthetic grounds by the new designer, Calvin Evans. In 1999, two more calendars were added to the range. The original has now been retitled the Rick Tomlinson Portfolio Calendar. It has been joined by a Wildlife Calendar and a Desk Calendar. This was a direct response to clients who wanted non-sailing images and smaller calendars. But it now means that each passing year requires thirty-six new images of the necessary quality. Every photo shoot becomes, at some level, a calendar shoot.

That Rothmans *would bury her bow on this breezy Sydney-Hobart run was inevitable. It was just a matter of how far – far enough to make a calendar image.*

Corum's *spinnaker floating so perfectly to leeward was a matter of pure chance. Good luck for both photographer and sponsor.*

This spinnaker at La Nioularque was backlit by the sun for the briefest moment

Lifeboat crews on a mission to provide action images, have been a great source of calendar photographs both for the RNLI and for Rick Tomlinson: Hayling Island Atlantic 21, Valentia Arun and (below) Dun Laoghaire Trent class lifeboats.

*Tall ships by Tower Bridge (Above Left), the village of Porto Cervo (Left)
and an Antarctic outpost (Above) – all provide glorious images using
the same time exposure techniques that Tomlinson introduced to
on-board photography.*

The J Class provided photographers with stunning visual images in the thirties.
They are still doing so 70 years later – but choosing a single calendar image is never
easy. Photograph Above: Endeavour, Left: Shamrock V and Below: Velsheda.

Calendar images from sailing expeditions to high latitudes;
Above Left: Alaska, above: Antarctica and below: Spitsbergen.

Below: Three bowmen aboard the massive New Zealand 'K' boat, 1988 Challenger for the America's Cup.

Far Left: Crew co-ordination highlighted on the 18 Foot Skiff, Xerox.

Middle Left: Rapscallion, Swan racing in Guernsey.

Left: Team EF in early training, and earlier graphics.

The French professional circuit led the way in bright graphics for their sponsors. Florence Arthaud and Pierre 1ER.

Chapter 4
The Card

The Whitbread Round-the-World Race 1989-90

January 1990 – Aboard the sailing yacht *The Card*.

'It was the restart in Auckland. And, as always in New Zealand, every man and his dog were out in anything that would float, from superyachts to canoes. The Card *was another Maxi, like* Drum, *but a two-masted ketch rather than a single-masted sloop. We'd started at the leeward end of the line. The authorities had created an exclusion zone, a corridor through the packed crowd of boats. We had* Rothmans *sailing slightly behind and to windward of us, and I was watching them, taking pictures, crouched on the side deck. They tacked away, and I remember looking round and seeing that we were sailing into the spectator fleet.* Rothmans *had chosen to stay in the corridor. Both options were allowed in the rules, but still, I was surprised that we were weaving through this wall of boats. I went back to taking pictures – I was a cameraman, not a tactician.*

'Then I heard the crash, behind me. Lots of noise, shouting, banging, all at once. I spun round with the camera up and fired away. The smaller mast, the mizzen, was coming down. It was over in moments. It'd caught the rigging of an anchored spectator boat as we sailed past. We didn't slow much. But the other yacht was much smaller, and we rolled him onto his side before the mizzen gave way. We broke free when it did. And there we were, one mast down within half an hour of the start, with about six thousand miles to go. It didn't feel real, it was as though it was happening to someone else. There was so much preparation and build-up to those starts, it was a huge disappointment.

'There was a lot of attention on us initially, as we cleared the mess up. But gradually the spectators drifted away, and we were left alone to figure out the next move. We dropped the broken mast over the side on a buoy, and carried on – pretty half-heartedly. The hope was that the mast could be repaired quickly and we could go back in for it. But after the shore team had picked it up, it was confirmed that it would take days, maybe weeks, to fix. So on we went, all the way through the Southern Ocean, round Cape Horn and up to Punta del Este, with one mast instead of two. Like a Ferrari in a Grand Prix with half the valves sticking.'

The Whitbread had crept up on Tomlinson while he had been working on the calendar. But with the first of those established, the next Whitbread was by now only a year away. Boats were beginning to be launched, teams were getting organised. *The Card* had been built in the United States, and arrived in England after her first trans-Atlantic crossing. The team was skippered by Roger Nilson, who had been the navigator aboard *Drum*. One of the watch captains was another *Drum* veteran, and a close friend – Magnus Olsson. The boat was headed down to the Mediterranean, to Majorca, for winter training – they wanted to know if Rick would be interested in joining them?

The offer was to sail as crew for the whole race. Everyone expected that the photographs Tomlinson would take would be useful, but that wasn't to be his primary role aboard the boat. It was a difficult decision. Should he leave the photography business and go back to sailing? Perhaps a compromise was possible; Rick went down to Majorca and made them an offer. He would sail two legs. The first was essential, to have pictures available as soon as possible. And racing down to Punta del Este from Southampton would provide the opportunity for photos in a variety of conditions. The next had to be a Southern Ocean leg, and Tomlinson chose the second. That would include the start in Auckland, the rounding of Cape Horn and the return to Punta del Este. Tomlinson argued that with a photographer on board, Nilson could provide much better coverage for the sponsor.

The Card *loses her mizzen mast at the Auckland restart.*

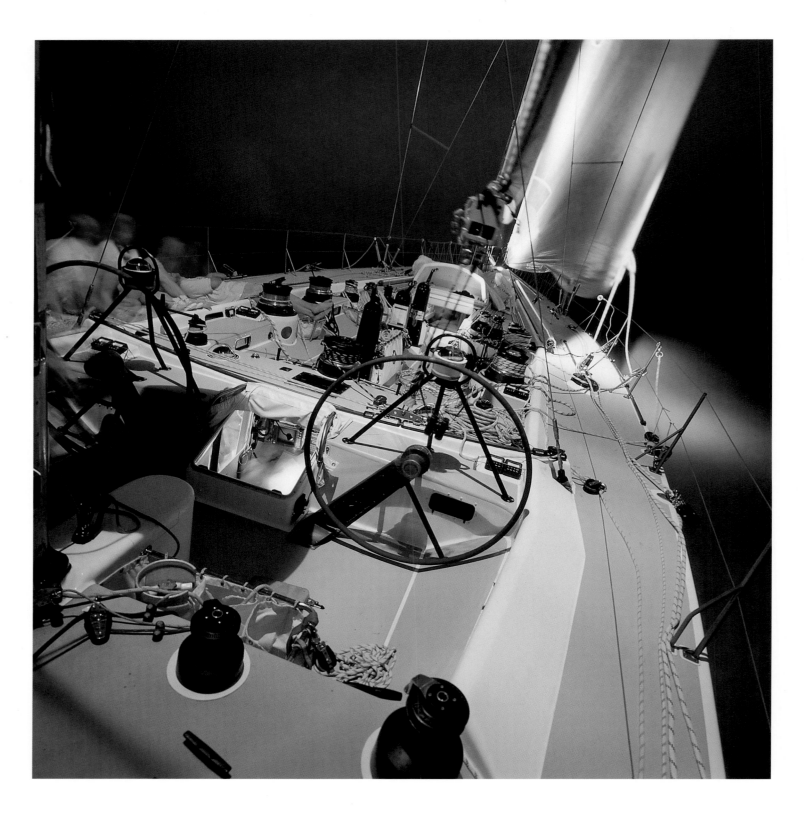

Nilson agreed, and Tomlinson set about his preparation, always looking for something new. *Seahorse* magazine had been approached by Penny Haire, who had an idea for taking aerial shots from boats. A kite would carry the camera aloft, along with the mechanism to fire the shutter remotely. *Seahorse* suggested to Haire that she talk to Tomlinson, who was enthusiastic. No one had got an image of a Whitbread boat racing hard, deep in the Southern Ocean, taken from off the boat. Anything that might get that picture was worth working on. Along with the kite, he packed a couple of cameras for this second race. One of them would be risked in the aerial efforts, and he more than doubled the amount of film for each leg, to fifty rolls.

And so Tomlinson came to be aboard *The Card* during its most famous moment – the photographer once again being photographed. There is some astonishing video footage of the incident, and the impact on the unfortunate spectator boat. For *The Card* it was an unmitigated disaster, in what was already developing into a pretty average performance. They were the last of the three ketches in the race, all of which had a clear advantage over the rest of the – sloop-rigged – fleet. *The Card* team watched Peter Blake and

Above: Light from the mizzen mast provides surreal illumination for this night shot.

Right: A headsail change, photographed from the mast at the first spreader.

his *Steinlager* crew win every leg, and dominate overall. But sailing that long Southern Ocean passage with a fraction of their true horsepower was the darkest moment.

This particular dark cloud came with a sliver of silver lining for Rick Tomlinson. With the full crew on board but only half the sail-handling, everyone had time on their hands. The incident had also brought media attention onto *The Card*, and a demand for pictures of the boat. He had plenty of time to experiment with the kite, with new camera angles, exposures and shooting techniques. Unfortunately, the kite camera didn't produce anything useful – this is probably the first ever publication of a picture from it. If there were to be Southern Ocean shots taken from off the boat, another way would have to be found. By the next race, there would be no question of anyone hanging around to fly a kite off the back of the boat.

The race was changing beyond the recognition of its pioneers. *Steinlager*'s utter domination of the event was thanks to a ruthless professionalism. Aboard *Drum* the crew had been given only a little pocket money to spend in port. On *The Card* there were more paid crew, but Rick was still expected to fund his photography by selling his pictures. The same system was in place, sending the photos to the magazines on-spec. He had some help in Sweden from Jeppe Wikstrom, who ran a picture agency in the boat's home country. Wikstrom represented Rick successfully throughout the race. But the approach to the media and sponsors, as well as the sailing, was due for an injection of some business principles. One of the men responsible for what was to come was aboard *The Card* on the long slog through the Southern Ocean and around Cape Horn. His name was Johan Salén, then a world-class windsurfer and adventurer. He would come to be a very successful Whitbread innovator and competitor, and one of Tomlinson's most important collaborators.

Left: Full power reaching, the Whitbread 1989-90 winner, Steinlager.

Above: Tracy Edwards and her crew aboard Maiden,
the first ever all-women team in the Whitbread.

The daily grind of life aboard The Card.

Early days of professional racing. The Card *and* Rothmans *training for the Whitbread.*

Leading the charge to professionalism, the New Zealand team a few miles away from the finish and their clean sweep of six legs and the overall prize in the 1989-90 Whitbread.

Chapter 5
RIBS and Helicopters

August 1991 – The North Sea.

'I'd been commissioned to photograph the Corum Sailing Team, who were then also the French Admiral's Cup team. They went on to win that regatta later that year. But this was earlier on in the season, in Nieuwpoort, Belgium. The Corum advertising people had this image in their heads of an aerial photo, with all three boats sailing downwind in line astern, with their spinnakers up. And we had all gathered, with a helicopter, to try and take the picture. Because they were racing that day, we had to do it first thing in the morning, about seven a.m. The fifty footer had only just arrived an hour earlier, having sailed through the night to get there. The last thing the crew wanted was to go out again for a photo shoot. But they were professionals, and understood the need.

'We got everyone out there more or less on time, but it was difficult from the start. The helicopter had no marine-frequency VHF radio on board, so we had to use my marine handheld in the helicopter, which wasn't easy with the engine and rotor noise. Fortunately, I had Lou-Lou Rendall (from Corum's PR agency) with me to do the talking, and she spoke good French. But communication was very difficult. It didn't help that the pilot's first language was Flemish. Time and again we tried to line them up for the spinnaker shot. But the different speeds of the three boats and the conditions made it impossible. One boat would get a puff of breeze and accelerate out of position, or the spinnaker would collapse – to be honest, it was a total nightmare. Tempers were fraying, so in the end we just told them to sail together as close as they could, upwind or downwind, and we'd shoot what we could see. That was how we got the image that Corum used. It was completely different to what they had in mind originally, but it worked perfectly and they loved it. But when you consider how much money was spent on getting everything together to take that picture, and how close we came to getting nothing at all – it makes me shudder even now.'

The end of Tomlinson's second Whitbread in May 1990 had got him thinking about buying his own photo chase boat. Back on the regatta circuit, he had been getting frustrated for some time with the limitations of press boats. He had learned a lot from being with the other, more experienced photographers in the early days, but press boats ploughed too reliable a furrow: from the start to the windward mark, then back to the leeward mark, and so on until the finish. The odds were high that everyone on board would get some decent shots that would keep magazine editors happy, but the odds were conversely low that anyone on board would get anything particularly special. Good and usable – yes; unique – no.

The problem was that those unique images were the calendar shots Tomlinson needed, and for which his business now had an inexhaustible appetite. But to get those pictures, it was necessary to take more chances. The boat had to travel around the course more, backing hunches as to where the action was going to happen. It was possible to be completely wrong, and to come off the water with nothing worth using. Equally, a break with the light, a man going overboard, a rig coming down, a wild broach – if it happened at the right moment, then the shot was worth a hundred run-of-the-mill images. Some luck was necessary, but it was a percentage game of being in the right place at the right time. Luck could be manufactured simply by sticking at it. With the greater control and flexibility of an independent boat, it was possible to be out on the course first, to come in last, and chase whatever chances might come around.

Apart from the pressure of the calendar, a lot more of his work required the greater freedom. The profile Tomlinson's photographs had achieved after another successful Whitbread, and a couple of calendars, meant that commissions were flowing in. All sorts of people commission photographers for all sorts of reasons – weddings are something that most of us are familiar with. In sailing, there are various interested parties, besides the magazines, who might want pictures. The sponsors or supporters of an individual boat

The Corum Sailing Team get lined up during a difficult photo shoot off Nieuwpoort, Belgium.

might want some images to make their marketing money work. If the event itself has a sponsor, they too will need pictures – for advertising the event or their products in association with the event. Just as for a wedding, they will call up a photographer and hire him or herself for the day, or perhaps the duration of the regatta. All the pictures the photographer takes in that time will belong to the person who commissions them – they will own the copyright. The alternative is that the photographer shoots on-spec – and so retains the copyright. Then each and every use of the picture has to be paid for separately. Despite the apparently high daily rates (remember all those overheads), owning the pictures ends up a lot cheaper for regatta organisers and sponsors than paying for each commercial use individually.

Tomlinson made the decision to go ahead with what was another major investment. The steady stream of commissions coming through the door had put his business on a solid footing. The insecurities of only shooting the regatta circuit on-spec for the magazines seemed to be behind him. He bought a 5.5 metre RIB with a 90 horsepower outboard engine, and an ageing four-by-four van to tow it with. This set-up got him just about anywhere in Europe that he had to get photos, from the Baltic to the Mediterranean. Its usefulness was quickly established by that 1991 commission to photograph the Corum Sailing Team. They had three boats of different sizes – a one tonner, a two tonner and a fifty footer – and they wanted pictures of them all, separately and together. For this assignment, he needed the RIB at the different regatta venues, to chase around the race course and get the right boat in the photos.

On these and many similar trips, Tomlinson took along his own driver. At Grand Prix events such as the Admiral's Cup, there's a lot of spectator traffic. Trying to drive the boat and take photos at the same time is a hazard to everyone else out there. Phil Harris, another veteran from Tomlinson's first two Whitbreads, has been a regular over the years. Outside Europe, however, shipping the RIB to events wasn't practical, which meant that for the USA, Australia, the Far East and elsewhere, Tomlinson was back on the press boat. If the shoot was commissioned and the press boat wasn't working, then chartering a boat, and sometimes a driver to go with it, was an option. But when push comes to shove, if you've absolutely, categorically, *got* to get the photo, there's only one way: a helicopter.

For most of us, riding in a helicopter is a never- or once-in-a-lifetime experience. For sailing photographers, it's the way they go to work. But it's not cheap. In Britain the cost was over six hundred pounds an hour by the end of the nineties. The safety regulations and the amount of emergency equipment required for helicopters to operate over water make it expensive. In the States the regulations aren't as prohibitive and the prices come down to as little as three hundred and fifty dollars an hour. Then there's the cost of getting to the race course. In the Solent area, the nearest helicopter is up to an hour and a half away. That's nine hundred pounds gone before a boat has even been sighted. At the same time, a photo used on a sailing magazine cover will earn around two hundred pounds – it'll cost four or five cover shots just to get the helicopter to the venue.

Left: This shot of Primagaz *took three trips to France before the conditions were right.*

Below: Although this image of Banque Populaire *and* Haute Normandie *was taken from a RIB, in seconds the boats will be gone, and only the helicopter can keep pace.*

As a consequence of these brutal financial realities, helicopters are usually restricted to commissioned work. Sometimes they are provided for the press corps by a regatta sponsor. They might be hired by a boat sponsor. Even then, there are still difficulties, as the Corum shoot demonstrated. And what if it's pouring with rain on the big day? But there are times when there's no other way to get the picture. The accelerating speed of modern race boats means those circumstances are turning up more and more often. Multi-hulls long ago made it impossible to keep up in any kind of powerboat stable enough for photography – unless it's more expensive to charter than a helicopter. The choices at a multi-hull race are stark: hire a helicopter, or sit two miles ahead of the start line and snatch four or five frames as the boats blast past.

The choice of perspective is also greater than from a boat. The photos from a helicopter at masthead height, backing away from a racing boat screaming downwind in twenty-five knots, cannot be taken from a RIB. Combine the height advantage with the speed at which the viewing position can be changed, and the lack of crowds, and the benefits of using a helicopter are obvious; for a big race start it cannot be bettered.

However, there are regulations about where it's possible to fly. For major events like the start of the Volvo Ocean Race, helicopters flying in the Solent are required to keep five hundred feet above the boats. Once out into the English Channel, they can do as they please. A lot of the helicopter chartering that goes on is for photography and film work of one type or another. As a consequence, many of the pilots will already know the best angles and positions. Tomlinson prefers Castle Air in Devon, ex-Navy pilots with exceptional flight training and film experience. The basic rules remain the same though – the first windward mark and the start are the optimum moments, and are best shot from one of the four quarters of the boat.

If the helicopter is now the ultimate photographic platform, planes offer a pleasantly cheaper alternative for some jobs. It's possible to swan around all day in a single-engined Cessna for the price of an hour in a helicopter. But, of course, once in the air, it's not possible to stop. On some occasions this can work well. A Cessna can wait all day at Tasman Island, near the end of the Sydney-Hobart Race, allowing the photographer to get a shot of each boat as it comes by, against the towering backdrop. With the right light and the right boat, it can be a classic photo – perfect, in fact, for a calendar.

While the J Class attracts much of the attention at the Antigua Classic Regatta, often the smaller yachts are having much of the fun. The helicopter is the only way to shoot both, especially in these conditions.

Left: This 18 Foot Skiff image was taken on a return trip from another shoot. Again proving the mobility of the helicopter and its unique perspective.

Above: With the Fastnet start scheduled for the late evening, a helicopter was booked with just this type of image in mind.

A low vantage point and long telephoto lens creates an unusual
perspective of the yachts in the fleet at Cork Week, and of Bank Raid
individually at the same regatta.

The way that sunshine reflects off wind-driven water always provides a dramatic setting for photographs taken from a helicopter:
Above: Stars and Stripes *and* Team New Zealand *racing prior to the 1992 America's Cup. Below:* Corum *at the Kenwood Cup.*
Top Right: France *and* Spain *during the 1992 America's Cup Challenger Series. Bottom Right:* Ronstan Ultimate Challenge *at the Kenwood Cup.*

Close up or distant, the platform helps determine the type of image.
Left: Ad Hoc *from a RIB at the Commodore's Cup;*
Above: Ausmaid *from a plane off Tasman Island in*
the Sydney-Hobart Race.

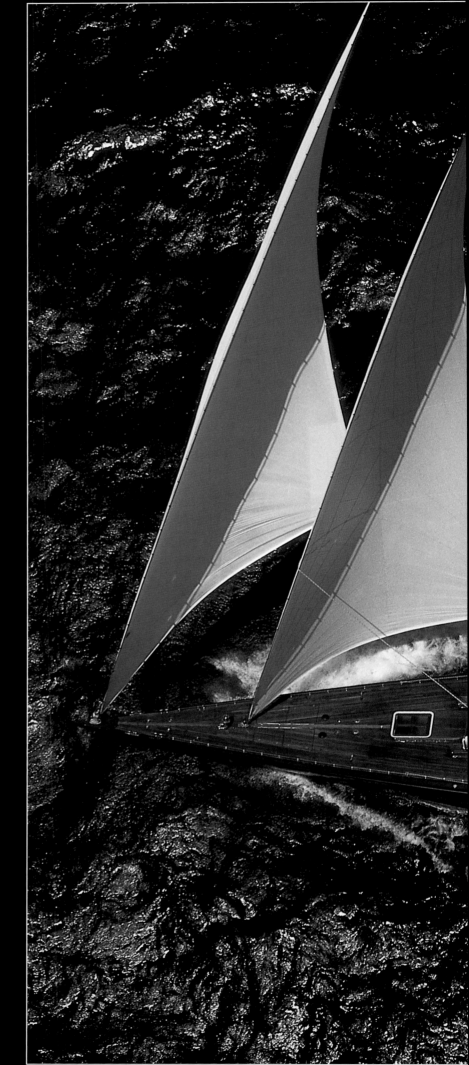

Above: English Braids *training for the Mini-Transat.*

Right: Endeavour, *crewed by Team New Zealand, brings together the past and the present of the America's Cup.*

Tracy Edwards and her Jules Verne crew, aboard
Royal SunAlliance.

Chapter 6
The Lifeboats

February 1992 – Lough Swilly, Ireland.

'The Mayday call was from a fishing boat. They had been struggling with engine problems all night. Having failed to get it going, they were being blown ashore at Fanad Head. That's to the west of where Lough Swilly emerges into the Atlantic, on the north-facing coast of Ireland in County Donegal. The lifeboat that got the call to attend was a D Class, a soft-bottomed inflatable, which was out with us on a photoshoot on Lough Swilly. We decided to follow them; it was a good opportunity to take some photos of a real rescue. As we neared the lough entrance it started to get rough; the northerly gale was pushing against a big spring tide running out of the lough, and had set up some serious overfalls. As soon as the lifeboat got into these standing waves, we could all see that they would get swamped; they couldn't get outside. My RIB was about the same size, but it had a hard bottom, and although it was a wild ride, with Nick Keig driving it was safe enough.

'Once we got outside the lough, it was nowhere near as rough as the entrance. There was a good breeze, but the sun was shining and it wasn't a bad day. The biggest problem was finding the fishing boat. The Coastguard were trying to direct us to him over the VHF radio, but we'd only come out for a couple of hours of photography with the lifeboat. We didn't have a chart, and we had no idea of the landmarks they were using in their descriptions, because we'd never been there before. There was another lifeboat on its way, a big offshore boat. But it would be a couple of hours before it arrived. Fortunately, the Coastguard managed to get us to them just in time. The fishing boat was about thirty feet long, aground and being washed onto the rocks under the cliffs, in breaking seas. We managed to get a line aboard them and pulled them off. The most exciting part was towing them back into the lough, through the surf in the entrance. Even on a really long tow-line they kept catching waves and overtaking us, which was a little scary. Once inside we handed them over to the lifeboat. The whole thing demonstrated how much more seaworthy the Rigid Inflatable Boats (RIBs) are, compared to the fabric-bottomed ones. After this rescue the RNLI changed that D Class boat for an Atlantic 21. And they gave Nick Keig and me a medal.'

Tomlinson's matter-of-fact account rather belies the experience and seamanship, not to say nerve, involved in the rescue. The fishermen were fortunate that he and Nick Keig were around. Tomlinson's connection with the Royal National Lifeboat Institute (RNLI) goes back to the Isle of Man, and continues to this day. He was a crewman aboard the Port St Mary lifeboat by the age of eighteen. New crew were usually invited to join by the local Coxswain, the skipper of the boat. There would be a crew practice once a week, and in the winter there were evening classes. Tomlinson remained with the Port St Mary lifeboat for five years, until the travelling and sailing meant that he was never at home for long enough to be much use.

It was Tom Power that rekindled the relationship, almost a decade later. Tomlinson had been working in Ireland for several companies that were sponsoring sailing. Some of the high-ranking individuals in the management of these companies were also involved in the hierarchy of the RNLI. Tom Power put the two things together and suggested that one of these companies might like to fund the creation of the RNLI's own photographic archive. The plan was to get pictures, at sea, of all of the twenty-eight lifeboats stationed around Ireland. Rothmans were enthusiastic, and would commission Tomlinson as the photographer. The pictures would remain with the RNLI, for use as images in all their printed material. The hope was that the overall benefit to the Institute would exceed the cost to Rothmans of commissioning the photographs. And this quickly proved to be the case, through the sale of their very successful calendars and merchandise.

The scheme was planned for the winter of 1991-92, when the weather should be appropriate for showing the boats in action. Nick Keig was enlisted as the RIB driver – and so it was that they came to be

Tyne Class, relief Lifeboat, stationed at Fleetwood.

afloat with the Lough Swilly lifeboat just when it would prove useful to some fishermen. It was one of many memorable moments in their journey round the coast of Ireland, through some of the most remote, exposed and beautiful country in Europe. They often visited isolated villages, where much of the community life revolved around the lifeboat. There they were quickly embraced by the locals, which gave them a privileged insight into the people and places.

The pair made four week-long trips with the RIB in tow, photographing one lifeboat each day. On arrival they would launch the RIB, which was often the most difficult part of the shoot. The lifeboat might be stationed on a rocky headland or beach, and the crew would be organised with whatever was necessary to get their lifeboat afloat. Getting the common-or-garden RIB in the water, even with Tomlinson's trusty four-wheel drive, was more of a challenge. Once afloat, they would head out to search for the roughest piece of water available. The lifeboat crews could be relied upon to ensure they were not disappointed. The visit was completed by the ritual consumption of prolific amounts of Guinness, the traditional conclusion to a lifeboat launch in Ireland. All very well, except that our heroic team were expected to participate every night of the week-long tours.

When the winter's work was complete, the RNLI got a chance to see the pictures, and they were delighted with the results. So delighted that the project was extended for another three years, to boats throughout the rest of the British Isles. Jameson Whiskey now came in as the sponsor. The schedule had to be altered for crews that didn't want to give up work on a weekday. Starting in the winter of 1992-93, the trips became away weekends. The departure was on a Friday evening, driving overnight to some far-flung lifeboat station. By ten o'clock the following morning, they would have the boats in the water for the first shoot. The RIB would be back on the trailer by lunchtime, and driven to the next venue to launch by two-thirty in the afternoon. That would have to be finished as darkness fell, when they would once again take to the road for

another sixty- or eighty-mile drive, before collapsing in a bed-and-breakfast. The RIB would have to be in the water again by ten o'clock the next morning. The Sunday's timetable would match the Saturday's, followed by the long drive home that evening.

It was a punishing schedule, and Tomlinson had to have someone along who could share the workload, driving the boat and vehicle, and launching and recovering the RIB. Alex Robson, Phil Harris or Ian Wilson, friends from the Hamble sailing community, have accompanied Rick on most of these trips. There were four weekends each winter, photographing a total of sixteen boats every year. The first three years were just as successful as the Irish venture, and the project was extended indefinitely. Apart from missing the occasional winter because of Whitbread Races, the shoots have gone on ever since, up and down the length and breadth of the British Isles. It's impractical to try to photograph every lifeboat, but sixteen boats a year provides the RNLI with a continually refreshed picture library. The work has also given Tomlinson the occasional precious photo for his own calendars.

The lifeboat commission isn't just hard work for the people, it's also demanding of the equipment. The picture of a heavy offshore lifeboat – airborne in a cloud of spray that reaches over the aerials – was taken from a twenty-foot open boat. With or without a rigid bottom, that's tough work for everything involved. The cameras take a pounding, and the work contributes to an attrition rate of about one camera body that's written off each year. Sometimes it's due to accumulated exposure to salt water, sometimes a single wave will do for the camera in one go. Marine photographers rarely use underwater cameras or waterproof housings. The fully waterproof, underwater cameras are designed with a wide-angle lens, which is not interchangeable. And the waterproof housings make it too difficult and slow to reload new film. Tomlinson uses a standard Nikon 35 mm, Single Lens Reflex (SLR) body, and a selection of demountable lenses. The only protection the camera gets is from his quick reactions – ducking out of the spray.

C Class Lifeboat,
off Redbay,
Northern Ireland.

21p · ISLE OF MAN

25p · ISLE OF MAN

37p · ISLE OF MAN

Main Photograph: Sennen Cove launch their Mersey Class lifeboat.

Inset Photographs: The RNLI was founded by Sir William Hillary in 1824 on the Isle of Man. For the Institution's 175th Anniversary, the Isle of Man Post Office commissioned Rick Tomlinson to photograph the island's five lifeboats for a set of commemorative postage stamps. The stamps feature, from Left to Right: Ramsey, Mersey Class; Douglas, Tyne Class; Peel, Mersey Class; Port Erin, Atlantic 75 Class and; Port St Mary, Trent Class lifeboats.

Left: A Trent Class, relief Lifeboat on station at Alderney in the Channel Islands.

Above: Hayling Island's Atlantic 21 gets airborne on Chichester Harbour Bar.

Fleetwood's Tyne Class, relief Lifeboat.

Top: Fishguard's Trent Class Lifeboat.

Above: Eastbourne's Mersey Class.

Left: Valentia's Severn Class.

D Class Lifeboat off Tramore, Ireland.

Chapter 7
High Latitudes

September 1998 – Arctic Ocean, Spitsbergen.

'We were visiting an old, abandoned hunting station in a remote part of the islands. Both our friends and the guides had briefed us about the polar bears, and before we went ashore we always had a good look around. For me, the whole purpose of the trip was to photograph polar bears, but it had to be done from a safe distance. For that reason, I'd borrowed a 600 mm telephoto lens from Nikon, worth about ten thousand pounds. We could see only one bear, about half a mile away from the hunting station. It's easy to think that polar bears are camouflaged for the Arctic ice, but they are also remarkably difficult to see on a mixed background of rock, grass and scrub.

'This was a dangerous place, so the skipper came ashore as well, staying on the beach to watch the bear. The guide climbed a small hill with us, for a better view of the area. Both of them were armed with a rifle and a pistol, and they each carried a radio to keep in touch. They took the danger from the polar bears very seriously, which was reassuring, because so did I. We had just got to the top of the rise when something made me look left – straight into the face of a bear that popped its head over a ridge about two hundred yards away. We knew that one bear half a mile off was one thing, but a second bear that close was definitely another. Still, old habits die hard, and my first reaction was to lift the camera and fire away.

'I must have shot a roll of film before I realised that the guide had indicated an orderly withdrawal. The polar bear was starting to move towards us. The slope was really steep, loose shale and grass, and we all tumbled down it pretty quickly. We were trying not to move too fast, because that would excite the bear. In theory it was a controlled exit, not a blind, panic-stricken flight. But once you got moving it was difficult to slow down. And with a fair amount of pace on, I clipped the lens against a rock. The impact tore it straight off the camera body and it crashed onto the ground. I wasn't in much of a position to go back and pick it up. That might have forced the guide to shoot the bear – he was covering our retreat with the rifle – which was the last thing I wanted. But I didn't particularly want to explain to Nikon that I'd lost the lens either. It would be hard enough taking it back broken. Fortunately, the person behind me had quick reflexes, and grabbed the lens as they slid past.'

The opportunity to travel to Spitsbergen had been the third such trip to high latitudes. It was the first that had started Tomlinson's interest in wildlife photography, beginning the chain of events that led to a calendar devoted to it. The first trip, like so many other parts of this story, had its roots aboard *Drum*. Three of the crew, during those long night watches, talked about what they would do after the race. They had dreamed of an expedition boat that could travel to the Antarctic. Unlike many other made-in-Whitbread plans, Skip Novak, Phil Wade and Chuck Gates had actually built their boat. Overseen by Novak, the fifty-three-foot *Pelagic* was constructed in steel in Southampton, and designed by another *Drum* crewman, Patrick Banfield.

The three had shared *Pelagic* at first, taking her for a year each. It was during Phil Wade's turn that Rick had his first taste of cruising in high latitudes. Novak completed his year with a refit for *Pelagic* in Cape Town. Phil Wade picked the boat up there, and headed west towards the tip of South America, planning to cruise up the coast of Chile before turning across the Pacific to New Zealand. Wade had invited Tomlinson to join the boat in Ushuaia, Argentina (just north of Cape Horn), during the southern hemisphere summer of early 1989. They had cruised north through the fjords of the Beagle Channel and into the Magellan Straits, Tomlinson leaving the boat in Porto Natales four weeks later. The trip was a taste of what long-distance cruising, in remote environments, could provide in the way of photographic opportunities. During that month, they had sailed through some stunning scenery, and taken memorable pictures of *Pelagic* in glacial ice, which were used in a calendar. This was landscape photography, but there was still a yacht somewhere in the image.

Seal colony in the Beagle Channel, Tierra del Fuego.

It was the next trip that put wildlife and landscape photography fully on the agenda. By 1992, *Pelagic* was solely Skip Novak's, and he was running her from Ushuaia as a charter expedition boat. The major customers were groups of climbers who wanted to get to Antarctica. Novak was a good climber himself, and he was acting as a guide as well as providing the transport and accommodation. It was January 1992; Rick and Cathie had recently moved into a new office in Port St Mary in the Isle of Man. Novak phoned from South America: he had just had a charter cancelled. He was trying to fill the boat with individual travellers who wanted to see the Antarctic wilderness – was Rick interested? The boat departed in ten days, and the cost would be five thousand US dollars. It was a good deal, as Tomlinson would be needed to help sail the boat across the notorious Drake Passage from Cape Horn to the Antarctic Peninsula. Rick was keen, Cathie was not – having taken on the new office, the business couldn't afford it. The five-week trip was a lot of time and money to sacrifice to speculative photography. Tomlinson said no, and went back to the work on his desk. But those empty calendar pages loomed large in his mind, and by lunchtime he had persuaded Cathie. He called Novak back to tell him he'd be there in time.

Once again, Tomlinson flew to Ushuaia to join *Pelagic*. In 1989, he had taken out replacement sail battens, carrying them in a protective plastic pipe as far as Buenos Aires. There he had transferred to a much smaller plane that couldn't carry the seven-metre tube. He had rolled the battens and left the pipe standing in a quiet corner of the airport. Three years later, as he retraced his steps, the pipe was still there, unmoved, gathering dust. It may be there still. On this occasion, the baggage allowance was taken up by Musto clothing – but more of that later. Novak had managed to fill the berths, but none of those aboard had much experience on a yacht. Inevitably, in such circumstances, Drake Passage was as wicked as its reputation threatened. It blew sixty knots, with accompanying huge Southern Ocean seas. They were debilitating conditions, and for the last half of the six-day passage, only Tomlinson and Novak were doing watches on deck, turn and turn about.

But it was an appropriate price to pay, to get to one of the most unique and remote areas in the world. With the rest of the guests just wanting to see the best of the landscape and wildlife, the trip quickly came to revolve around Tomlinson's photography. They saw penguins, whales, skuas and yet more penguins. The wilderness environment was stunning, and Novak's experience and ability allowed Tomlinson to make the most of the opportunity. Novak would lead on some gentle ice climbs, and belay Tomlinson while he struggled up behind. They explored ice caves on foot, and sailed amongst the bergs and growlers aboard *Pelagic*. The photographs were remarkable, and filled many calendar pages.

It was to be six more years, however, before Tomlinson was to return to quite such high latitudes, on another speculative journey in search of calendar images. This voyage, north to Spitsbergen, had started with a party for the visit of a cousin of Tomlinson's girlfriend, Annika. Rick had met Annika in Gothenburg in 1997 – during the preparation for Team EF's Whitbread Race – they married early in 1999. Other guests that evening had mentioned that they were taking their cruising boat to Spitsbergen during the coming summer. Per-Magnus had been a guide on the island for a number of years, and offered to help them see the place properly. Tomlinson was enviously enthusiastic, and it turned out that Per-Magnus was also taking a party – mostly composed of family members – up there at the end of the summer. The trip was to be aboard a converted working boat; originally built in 1953, it was now a hardy expedition charter boat. It was an ideal opportunity to get photos for the second wildlife calendar. By the early hours, and several bottles of red wine later, Annika and Rick were going too.

They flew to Spitsbergen, via Oslo and Tromsø, to join the boat. Spitsbergen is the main island of a group that is part of the Svalbard archipelago, governed by Norway and situated high above the Arctic Circle, six hundred miles from the North Pole. Polar bears would be an ever-present opportunity, as well as a danger, and the guides were always armed when the party went ashore. Tomlinson's research had led him to believe that the best chance of photographing the bears safely was on the ice floes that gathered off the east coast of the islands. It should be possible for the ship to get close enough to allow him to get his pictures unharmed, and without startling the bears into the water. But the longer and more powerful the lens, the better the

Polar dolphins in the Southern Ocean.

chance of good photos. His own equipment topped out at a 300 mm lens, so he went to Nikon to ask about something more suitable. When professional photographers have a track record of buying and using Nikon equipment, the company are prepared to lend specialist items on an occasional basis. Nikon agreed to let him take their brand new, 600mm telephoto lens. It was almost a metre long.

The first opportunity to use it to get the pictures that Tomlinson wanted came just where he expected – a bear was spotted on an ice floe on the eastern side of the archipelago at five o'clock in the morning. The twenty-four-hour-daylight was soft that early; it was the perfect opportunity. But the large male bear, unnerved by the approach of the ship, flopped into the ocean before Tomlinson could get many pictures. Another opportunity came soon after, when a mother and two cubs were spotted together. The family were much less willing to take to the water, and for half an hour Tomlinson was free to photograph the trio at his leisure, without stressing the animals. He used fifteen rolls of film in thirty minutes, taking every frame several times, at different exposures and apertures – bracketing, as it's called – to make sure he got what he wanted.

And so, when he was threatened by the bear a couple of days later, the 600mm lens had already done its work. Tomlinson's experience on the Spitsbergen island remains one of his most frightening, and memorable. Bringing back Nikon's ten-thousand-pound lens damaged paled into insignificance in contrast. Fortunately it was only the mount and not the glass of the lens itself that was broken. The repair was straightforward, and Nikon happy with the compensatory photograph of a polar bear!

Above: Gentoo penguins, Antarctica.

Below: Harbour seal basks on an Alaskan ice floe.

Right: A polar bear pops its head above a ridge line.

Timoneer *anchored in Ford's Terror, a fjord in Alaska.*

Above: Brown bear in Alaska.

Below: Polar bear in Spitsbergen.

Top Right: Killer whale in Alaska.

Bottom Right: Dolphins in Timoneer's wake in Alaska.

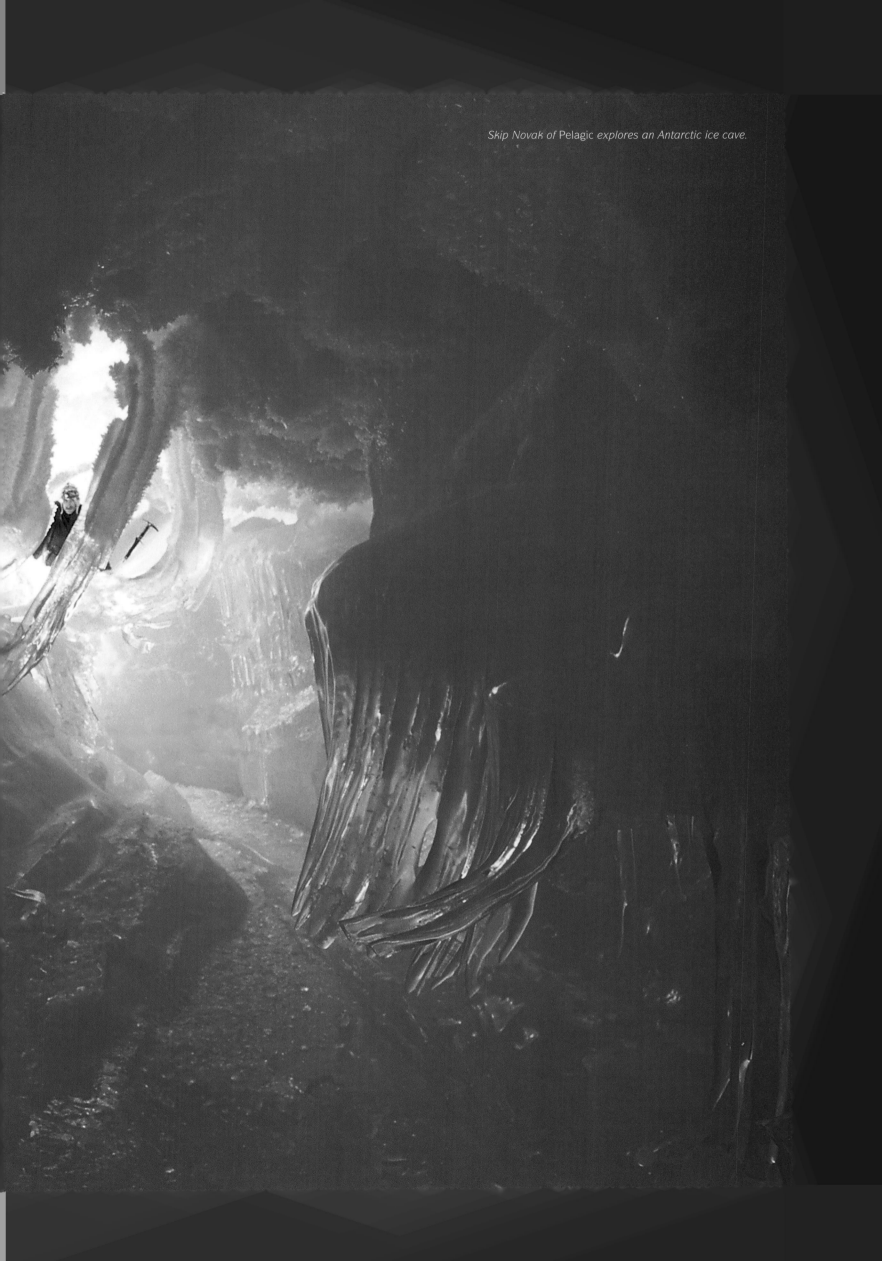

Skip Novak of Pelagic *explores an Antarctic ice cave.*

British Antarctic Survey vessel, the James Clark Ross.

Timoneer and a Harbour seal, sharing Alaskan sunlight.

A Humpback whale chooses the perfect moment –
soft light, flat water – to break the surface.

Chapter 8
Intrum Justitia

The Whitbread Round-the-World Race 1993-94

February 1994 – Aboard the sailing yacht *Intrum Justitia*.

'I had all the equipment necessary to send pictures from the boat. No one had done anything like that in those days; we were the first. But the technology, while adequate in theory, was pretty marginal in practice. This particular occasion was deep in the Southern Ocean. It all sounded under control on deck, and I had a clear run at the galley – breakfast was finished and there was an hour or more before lunch. It was a good opportunity to try and process some film. I pulled out the little fishing box I kept the gear in, and used the changing bag to get the film out of the cartridge and into the developing tank. Once the process was started, it had to be finished. The film had three minutes in the developer, kept at twenty degrees – not easy with no heater and the air temperature just above zero. Then the film was washed, put into a bleach fixing solution for two more minutes, and then given a final five-minute wash.

'Everything was quiet when I started. But, of course, as soon as I was committed a squall hit us. I could hear and feel the boat going faster and faster. There were shouts from up top, then a bang as the spinnaker blew out, and a call for all hands on deck. I couldn't leave the film without ruining it. And I really didn't want to lose the pictures, they were some of the best so far. So I stuck at the galley. The next thing I know there's wet, shredded spinnaker everywhere. Marco, the sailmaker, is fumbling around trying to get the sewing machine out to fix it. Magnus has decided that he might as well make lunch, since everyone is now up. And I'm in the way, trying to avoid poisoning the whole crew, and keep the timing about right. It was chaos, but somehow the chemistry worked.

'I put the film to dry in the engine box, above the generator. I left it there and went on deck for my watch. Four hours later, I got back down and found my precious negatives floating in the bilge. So I borrowed the sailmaker's blower and got them dry again. I was tired, but lucky that the navigator, Marcel van Triest, was enthusiastic about what I was doing. He didn't mind giving up space in his 'office' for me to try and send the photographs. I had to hold the Nikon scanner in my hands to iron out the bumps and stop it jumping. It took several attempts to get a decent picture into the computer, before translating it into a file that could be sent by modem over the satellite communications. I think it still took another two hours to get a single image out – an exhausting business. During the whole race, we managed to send maybe ten or twelve photographs off the boat. But they were the only ones like it. And they were used in newspapers around the world.'

The exposure that just those few photographs provided to the sponsor would probably have been enough to justify Tomlinson's principal role on the boat as a cameraman. The Whitbread Race, in its sixth running, had changed. Now it was as much about measurable media return as it was about winning. In both contexts, *Intrum Justitia* was a model entry. It had been put together by Johan Salén, the project manager, with Roger Nilson as skipper and Magnus Olsson as a watch captain. Intrum Justitia were the sponsors, a major European debt collector – in itself a comment on the changes that had taken place in the world since 1989, when the sponsor had been a credit-card company. Along with the other Swedish watch captain Gurra Krantz, Nilson and Olsson were joined by one crewman for each of the European countries in which Intrum Justitia had offices. With each individual promoting the boat in their home country, even the crew structure was part of the media campaign.

This time, Salén, Nilson and Olsson wanted Tomlinson along for the whole race, primarily to take

North Atlantic blast reaching, just as tough as the Southern Ocean.

pictures, both still and video. This Whitbread would be a one-year photographic assignment, rather than a return to full-time sailing. But putting so much effort into one project was still a risk, despite *Intrum Justitia* flying him home from the stopovers to attend to his business in Britain. Several things convinced Tomlinson that it was worth doing. The opportunity, during the racing, to send images off the boat was a big factor. The growth of interest in the race gave him confidence in a demand for the pictures. And, finally, there was the structure of the deal made by Tomlinson and Salén. It was a major component in making *Intrum Justitia* one of the most successful Whitbread projects ever.

For the first time, a Whitbread campaign would be commissioning Tomlinson as in-house photographer for the whole race. *Intrum Justitia* would pay for it all, providing the images free of charge to the world's media to ensure coverage for the sponsorship. Jeppe Wikstrom was involved again, using the photographic agency he was now part of – Pressens Bild – to distribute the pictures. Commercially, it was a runaway success, generating phenomenal coverage for the boat. But things didn't come together on the water until the second leg. Skipper Roger Nilson left at the end of the first leg. A knee injury forced him back to Sweden for treatment, and he was not asked to return. He was replaced by Lawrie Smith, who, with his small-boat experience and hard-driving style, was much more attuned to the needs of the race's new Whitbread 60

Above: Green Marine's composite team laminate Intrum Justitia's *inner skin of Kevlar – a material used throughout the boat in hull, ropes and sails.*

Left: A good moment to blow out a spinnaker, at least for the photographer.

class – shorter and more responsive than the old Maxis. *Intrum Justitia* came a narrow second overall behind Ross Field's *Yamaha*, and won all the Southern Ocean legs.

The electric performance of the Whitbread 60 made it both a more interesting photographic platform than the Maxi and a more demanding one. With only twelve crew aboard, there was a lot less time for taking pictures. Tomlinson had to rely on his experience to make the most of his opportunities. The equipment he took aboard was another ratchet up from the previous race. To the two Nikon bodies, he added a splashproof compact camera. He took fifty rolls of film for each leg – remembering that this time he sailed on all but one of them. He also took three lenses: a 16 mm, a 20 mm and an 80-200 mm telephoto.

Using this equipment Tomlinson had developed a portfolio of reliable set-ups. There are not that many places to take photographs from on a sixty-foot-long sloop – essentially, the front, the back, the top of the mast and the end of the spinnaker pole. The most consistent opportunities for good images come from standing behind the helmsman, preferably in heavy weather, with water coming over the bow; standing at the shrouds and using them for support in similar conditions; out at the end of the spinnaker pole with the 16 mm fish-eye lens; and the long-exposure night shots which are taken with the camera on a tripod or a clamp. After trying everything from one second to an hour, Tomlinson has a good feel for what the different exposure times will produce.

The night-time shots work best in stable conditions. Otherwise, Tomlinson's motto is 'average conditions make average photographs'. It's easy to think that the best time to reach for the camera is when everything is quiet and under control, and certainly mirror conditions can reveal a stillness and underlying tension. But it's the extreme conditions, with the crew hard at work, that create the memorable images. In a breeze, headsail changes are always dramatic affairs, with people in exposed positions on the bow. But arriving on deck with a camera at all the moments of maximum chaos is a good way to get on the wrong side of a short-handed, hard-pressed crew. That's when Rick's easy-going and amenable personality is a great asset.

The *Intrum Justitia* race remains Tomlinson's favourite Whitbread. It didn't hurt to come second, or twice to break the twenty-four-hour mono-hull distance-sailed record. But essentially it was a 'golden' moment in the development of the sport. The organisation was professional, while the pressures for success that big money programmes bring had not yet fully developed. The combination of crew and sponsor, management and support team was perfect. And everyone seems to have agreed – eleven of the thirteen crew that sailed aboard *Intrum Justitia*, along with many of the support staff, were to return for the next race.

Previous Pages: Intrum Justitia *at speed, on her way to setting the first of two world distance records for a 24 hour run – 423.3 nautical miles.*

Left: Early sea trials off the Isle of Wight give the first indication of the potential performance of the Whitbread 60.

Right: A potential later explored to the limits in the Southern Ocean.

Below: Night-time sail trimming on Leg 1.

*Caught with the spinnaker up in extreme conditions,
early morning in the Southern Ocean.*

Chapter 9
Shooting Briefs

October 1997 – Hayling Bay, England.

'We were taking pictures for a catalogue for Proctor, the mast-maker. Ironically, we'd gone to Hayling Island Sailing Club for the waves that set up on the bar at the entrance to Chichester Harbour. We didn't want to use rough water for all the shots, but it did give us the best prospects for some action photos. I had the art director for the shoot – from Proctor's advertising agency – driving the RIB for me. We went out with an International 14 dinghy. The waves had picked up with the ebb tide flowing out of the harbour into a fifteen-to-twenty-knot south-westerly breeze – classic Hayling conditions, the reason we were there. The 14 went upwind, out through the channel, the boat jumping clear of the water. It was fantastic stuff, and I knew I'd got some great material. The 14 turned around to run back downwind in the surf, and we turned and went with them. The waves were big, but a good length, and the 14 had no trouble with them. I can remember seeing this particular wave build behind us, and thinking it was going to be special when the 14 started surfing.

'Then the wave got to us, and I realised that we had a problem. It was big, we could accelerate down the face, with the risk of pitch-poling, or do nothing and spin the RIB sideways and broach. In the end, we did half and half, with the worst possible result. The boat rolled, dumping us both into the water. It was a surprise more than anything. I'd been out in much worse conditions and felt completely safe in that RIB. And then it capsized so easily and so quickly. Neither of us were hurt, but the boat was upside down, and the water was grey and cold. I had two cameras round my neck and a pocket full of exposed film – the day's work. I'd put each exposed film back into its container, in my left-hand jacket pocket, so I zipped that up. I thought about dropping the cameras; the weight wasn't making the swimming any easier. But all the shots of the 14 wave-jumping were still inside. I wanted those pictures. So I hung the cameras on the propeller, which was sticking up in the air like a coat rack.

'The 14, meanwhile, had just accelerated out of the way of the wave with no problem at all. Which was exactly what we should have done. They went over to a sailing cruiser going out of the channel, and asked them if they could help. The cruiser contacted the Coastguard, who got one of the local commercial RIB rescue teams to come out and tow us back in. It didn't rate a lifeboat attendance, as we were in no danger – just cold and wet. I think that if we'd had to, we could have righted the RIB by deflating the tubes on one side. But it was incredibly stable upside down, unsurprisingly, sitting on a big air bag with no keel. We towed the RIB in that way up, and the yard righted it the next day with a crane. Everything had fallen out: the whole camera bag and all the boat gear, like radios, flares, anchor and tool box. The only thing I had left was the cameras with the wave-jumping photos, and a pocket full of film. The film containers are pretty much waterproof, so all of that was safe. But I was worried about the film in the camera, as the camera was full of seawater.

'I figured that the best thing was to keep it wet until I could get it into the developing solution. So once we got ashore I dropped the camera in a bucket of water, and drove home with it like that. Then I used the changing bag from Intrum Justitia to get the film out of the camera and into a developing tank. I filled that with fresh water, and rinsed it a few times, then took the whole lot to the film processors, and explained the problem. They managed to develop the negatives, and the shots were great. But they needed to be, it was an expensive day's work. Apart from all the lost gear, the engine had to be completely rebuilt. It was a big claim, but the insurance company were fantastic – although I had a lot of explaining to do! – and I had new cameras from Nikon in a few days.'

Tomlinson's magnetic attraction for adventure extended even into the cultivated world of advertising.

An 18 Foot Skiff photographed for Hyde Sails.

The work had started back in 1992, with his first commission from Calvin Evans at CE Marketing. Evans had seen Tomlinson's pictures in the magazines, and called him to find out more. In particular, he wanted to know if Tomlinson was interested in taking some photographs of sailing clothing, on location, for the Musto catalogue. Tomlinson was, and the clothing was duly dispatched to his office. Rick was about to fly down to join *Pelagic* for the trip to the Antarctic. It made sense to take the clothing with him, in the hope that those aboard the yacht could be persuaded to model it in the icy landscapes.

Above: Luck helps: these dolphins popped up on cue, as the helicopter arrived for a Prout catamaran shoot off the Bahamas.

Left: The illusion of advertising: the palm branch framing the Prout catamaran off a Florida beach was held by the Art Director.

At the airport, the bill for the excess baggage – twelve cases of clothing – came to over twelve hundred pounds. So Tomlinson ditched all his personal stuff, and took just the Musto clothes and his camera gear. The dreadful conditions on the passage across to the Antarctic Peninsula gave him plenty of opportunity to get action shots of the foul-weather gear. The other guests on *Pelagic* built snowmen for him, modelling the casual clothes. And Skip Novak agreed to jump into the freezing sea wearing the bright yellow one-piece survival suit. At which point, a large leopard seal slid into the icy water nearby, apparently attracted by the idea of a lemon-flavoured human. Novak stayed in the water.

Tomlinson's time at Strategic Advertising had once again come in useful, having given him a solid foundation in the advertising business. He understood the process of brochure and advert production, from conception to print. He knew what was required from the photographer. And after that first shoot, the work started to roll in steadily. CE Marketing remains a major commissioner of Tomlinson's time, while the images sold to magazines for editorial use still act as their own advertisement for Tomlinson's work, attracting the attention of both potential clients and their agencies – just as they had with Calvin Evans.

Tomlinson's skills were particularly suited to, and he has come to specialise in, location shoots for manufacturers' new boats, and charter yachts. It's a very different job, however, to photographing yacht racing, where it's essential to watch and understand the flow of action. That understanding gives the pictures their context and meaning. Advertising is all about preparation of the image, about creating the right look for the product. Cruising boats aren't sold with pictures of a ten-man crew working flat out on deck. They're sold with lifestyle shots: drinks at sunset in quiet, secluded anchorages; pleasant sailing. It's the job of the advertising agency to decide on the precise image to match the potential market of the boat. They must then communicate those ideas to the photographer, perhaps through sketches or storyboards. But the photographer has to understand what's required, and deliver it. At times that can be frighteningly basic: cleaning off factory dust from a new boat. Tomlinson has found himself scrubbing the waterline alongside a well-paid art director on more than one occasion. On other occasions it's been a little more subtle – like having the right title of magazine lying on the saloon table.

On one occasion, during the 1993-94 Whitbread Race, Tomlinson was flying between a stopover port and the UK. He had arranged to photograph a catamaran in Fort Lauderdale en route, which underlines how important it was for him to get back to take care of other business. It also demonstrated how illusory those glowing lifestyle shots can be. To get the appropriate 'sundowners on deck' image, Evans had to hold the palm tree leaves in place while Tomlinson took the carefully framed photo to include the few feet of beach. The 'secluded beach' was actually a strip of sand beside Fort Lauderdale's main channel into Florida's network of inland waterways. And all the while, the pair were being eaten alive by mosquitoes.

Luck plays its part as well. On another shoot for the same client during the next Whitbread Race, a helicopter had been chartered to take some aerial shots of the catamaran sailing in the turquoise waters off the Bahamas. Just as Rick and the helicopter arrived from Fort Lauderdale, a school of dolphins popped up

and swam on the bow wave of the boat. Those moments can't be bought, or organised. On another occasion, Tomlinson found himself cooling his heels in an island jail for a few hours, after falling foul of a late change of venue. They only had the right paperwork for the previous location. This small problem aside, the Caribbean region offers a lot of advantages. It may seem an expensive luxury to arrange these photographic assignments in places like the Bahamas, but the sums make a lot of sense. With so many people involved on the day, disastrous weather can be expensive. Compared to the cost of delay, the price of a handful of tickets to Florida gets cheaper. The water is bluer, the weather almost certainly better, and the dolphins may even co-operate – if not local officialdom.

Marine clothing remains the other staple of Tomlinson's advertising work. The industry has seen some substantial changes in the nineties. No one is now likely to ship the clothes to the photographer and expect the pictures a month or two later. The product comes complete with models, locations and the art direction to match pop culture brand names. The sailing leisure wear that used to be tucked into a couple of pages in the back of the foul-weather gear catalogue now has its own glossy, stylised advertising and marketing material. But the sailing shots for the technical foul-weather clothing remain the same. And Tomlinson is happy enough to concentrate his work in this area. If you can't end up swimming while taking the picture, it just doesn't have the right buzz about it.

Pictures Left: After waiting all day for wind, a faint breeze arrived at the magic hour, just before sunset. Enabling a successful conclusion to the Bowman and Trintella advertising shoot.

Below: Musto's Volvo Ocean Race clothing is photographed in a more relaxed setting than the race itself will allow.

Pacific Wave *(Above)* and Bamsen *(Below)* photographed for advertising brochures with just enough action to be interesting – but not scary.

Right: Focusing on the product – an image for a sailmaker's advertising material.

Interior shots for advertising boats always require careful preparation and lighting. A Hallberg Rassy (left), the custom built Pacific Wave (above) and Timoneer (below).

Below: Selling the lifestyle is as important for the charter brochure of a custom boat like Pacific Wave, *as it is to the manufacturer of a production boat like the Najad (Right).*

Next Pages: An imaginative and eye-catching image is always part of the unspoken brief. The sailmaker's logos give it value to the client.

An exceptional day in the Solent ...

... while the Mediterranean is much more reliable.

This spectacular image of an International 14 was salvaged from a dangerous situation – the photo boat capsized moments after the shot was taken. The dinghy remained upright to co-ordinate the rescue.

Chapter 10
Magazine Assignment

1995 – Aboard the sailing yacht *Timoneer*, Southern Alaska

'We were chasing a pod of killer whales, trying to get photos of them as they surfaced. They were headed up a fjord, and it was difficult for Timoneer *to follow. A 120-foot superyacht isn't the most manoeuvrable of craft in close confines. The obvious answer was to get in the tender, a ten-foot RIB. With one of the crew as driver, we headed off to get closer. What we didn't realise was that the killer whales were hunting salmon. They do it in a pack, corralling the fish into a dead-end – just like the fjord we were following them up. Once the salmon were trapped, they moved in for the kill.*

'The result was a pretty terrifying feeding frenzy, which just erupted out of nothing, right in front of us: a mass of thrashing, writhing fins and churning water as the whales jumped in amongst the fish. We were much too close. As the action subsided – the salmon had either escaped or were dead – the whales turned and started nosing at the RIB. A ten-foot boat doesn't feel a particularly safe platform when it's being sniffed at by a twenty-foot killer whale – or two. It was pretty unnerving, although we were confident that the killer whale doesn't attack man. And as long as the RIB stayed the right way up, we were fine. I didn't end up in the water with them, didn't get wet, and I didn't lose my camera gear. The whales eventually lost interest and swam back off down the fjord. And I got the pictures.'

After the trip aboard *Pelagic* in 1992, Tomlinson had decided to do at least one major wildlife assignment each year. The 1993-94 Whitbread had immediately derailed that plan, but in 1995 he got back on track, in some style. Phil Wade had moved on to become the skipper of a 120 foot superyacht called *Timoneer*. The boat had been in San Diego for the America's Cup in 1995, and was now sailing up the coast in preparation for a cruise in the waters of Southern Alaska. Wade invited Tomlinson to join them for part of the research trip. Rick would be able to take photographs while the crew looked into the cruising potential of the region. It was also the kind of journey that might make an excellent magazine feature. If he could sell it as such, then this wouldn't have to be another purely speculative calendar venture like the *Pelagic* voyage.

Tomlinson flew out to Canada, joining *Timoneer* prior to her departure from Vancouver Island. They sailed slowly north to Juneau, the capital of Alaska. Using cruising guides, travel guides and pilot books, they were able to search for photographic opportunities in a way that's impossible for the land-locked. Aboard the yacht, the crew were a part of the environment twenty-four hours a day. There was no separation from it, no return to the hotel and cushioning civilisation. That proved the key to the success of the trip. It must be admitted, however, that a 120 foot superyacht did allow them to maintain this link with nature in some comfort.

They were surrounded by activity, which taught Tomlinson the frustrations of wildlife photography. Whales didn't provide any warning, they came and went in a moment, and Tomlinson missed several opportunities. He stuck with the same principles he used in his sailing work. He played the percentages, and kept putting himself in places where he might get the picture. Seeing the whales lift their tails lazily into the air started to feel almost commonplace. And he knew that eventually he would get the shot. And when he did, it was one of those truly special opportunities: a whale sounding, water streaming off its tail into the mirror surface of the sea, in soft, late-evening light.

On other occasions the images came almost too easily. The books told them that brown bears were known to fish at a particular waterfall. Tomlinson went there with Phil Wade, who set himself up to fish downstream. Tomlinson settled in for a long wait, which lasted less than five minutes. A brown bear arrived and, just like the book had suggested, was intent on dinner. The bear was trying to pull salmon out of the waterfall as they travelled upstream to spawn. The animal went straight into the water, caught a fish, and posed to eat it on a rock only ten metres in front of Tomlinson. The only attention the bear paid to the photographer was to

Victoria Falls.

look up at the sound of the motor drive. Unlike polar bears, a well-fed brown bear is unlikely to be a danger to man. Which was probably fortunate, because when it had finished its own meal, the bear wandered downstream. Rick watched with some concern, unable to warn Phil without alarming the bear. Wade was forced to leave the rod and retreat to the tree-line, and the bear moved on without further incident.

The three weeks cruising Alaska's South-East Passage were some of the most productive of Tomlinson's career. The photographs filled five magazine feature articles – one major advantage of magazine work being that the same material can be reused in different countries. It also supplied the whole of the first issue of the Wildlife Calendar, and several pages of the Portfolio Calendar. It was followed, a year later, by another trip that was just as successful. This came about from an apparently dead hour spent wandering around the back of the London Boat Show. Tomlinson came upon a sign, written by hand with a magic marker, on a piece of A3 paper. It said, 'Sail with the Elephants'. To someone with a passion for boats and wildlife, that was an irresistible draw. Tomlinson asked the people on the stand what it was all about. The company was Sail Safari, and it was promoting flotilla sailing holidays on Lake Kariba. A huge freshwater lake on the Zambezi River, covering over five thousand square kilometres, this was originally created by the Kariba Dam. Sited on Zimbabwe's northern border, the lake's shores included the Matusadona National Park.

It didn't take Tomlinson more than a few minutes to decide that he wanted to go. Again the topic seemed appropriate for a magazine feature article, particularly after the success of the *Timoneer* story. This was another aspirational cruise, which readers could dream about in those long winter evenings. If he could get the article commissioned, it would guarantee a use, and payment, for the material – and he might subsequently get a deal on the holiday. Since Tomlinson was at the Boat Show, he headed straight for the *Yachting World* stand. The magazine was intrigued by the cruise, and quickly offered to commission the story. On hearing the news, Sail Safari was more than happy to have Tomlinson and a writer along as guests, in exchange for the publicity the article would bring. The whole thing had taken less than a morning to get going – and all Tomlinson had been doing was burning some spare time. But it's the kind of result that only someone with a long and successful track record will get.

And so it was that Tomlinson found himself flying to Africa. The boats were carefully adapted Tiki 30s, a James Wharram-designed catamaran. They were locally built in plywood, using a simple construction and rig that looked entirely at home in the photographs. Sail Safari's concept was that the sailboats allowed for a silent, unthreatening approach to the animals. Tomlinson already knew of the advantages of living this way within a wilderness environment, and he was not disappointed. The shallow draught of the craft allowed them right into the shore with safety. Tomlinson saw and photographed elephant, hippopotamus, buffalo and impala. They heard the roar of lions, but didn't see them. Felt the bump of the occasional hippo under the boat at night. And they took some very hurried swims, thanks to the threat of crocodiles. For two years running, he had managed to complete a wildlife expedition – the planned assignments were back on track. But the Whitbread was looming again.

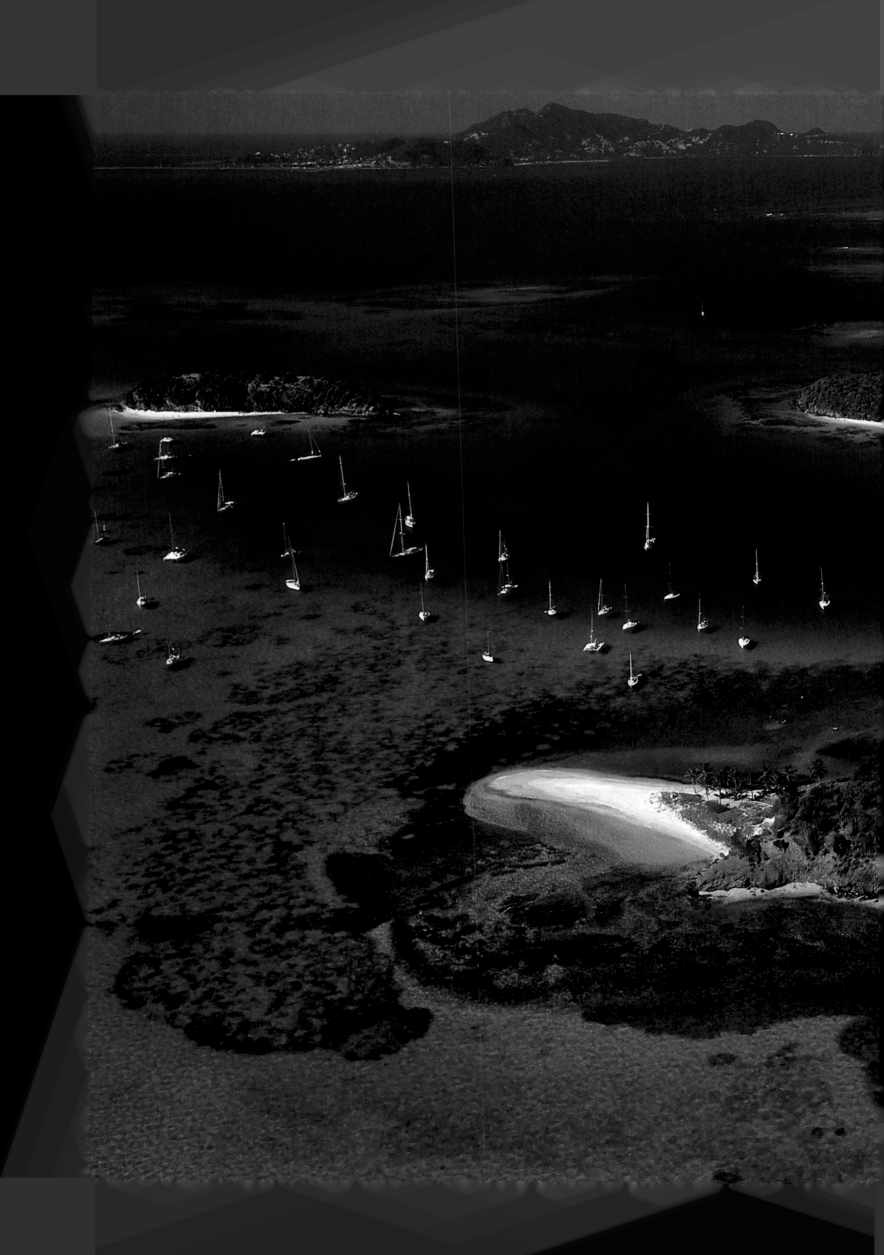

Previous Pages: Idyllic anchorage in the Tobago Cays.

These Pages: A brown bear salmon-fishing in Alaska.

Next Pages: Timoneer *manoeuvres for the photographer in glacier ice,
Tracy Arm, Alaska. If the journey is part of the magazine story, then images
of the boat are essential.*

Previous Pages: A Lake Kariba boat safari captured at dusk.

These Pages: The Lake Kariba boat safari allowed close but safe access to large and normally dangerous African wildlife: hippopotamus, elephants and crocodiles. A great idea for an article, combined with great images.

*A solitary penguin enjoys the stunning Antarctic
scenery and a brief moment of polar sunshine.*

Chapter 11
The Final Whitbread

The Whitbread Round-the-World Race 1997-98

June 1997 – The National Geographic Society, Washington, USA

'I'd flown out to Washington for the meeting with the National Geographic. *Although I'd been talking to them for about a year, I'd only been given the assignment recently, and I'd never been to their office. I got a cab about two hours early, because I was worried about being late. It was very hot, especially in a blazer and tie. So I was looking for somewhere with some air conditioning, or at least some shade, while I waited. I ended up drinking coffee in a café, which I don't think did anything to calm my sense of anticipation.*

'The building is imposing from the moment you see it. And as soon as you get inside, there's an instant sense of history. Bruce McElfresh was the picture editor for my story, and he showed me round the building and all the different departments. They have a huge workshop in the basement, where they build custom equipment for expeditions. One of the technicians asked me if there was anything I needed. I felt like James Bond on his trip to see Q before the big mission. When I said no, I wasn't sure who was more disappointed, me or him.

'The whole place had the atmosphere of a library: an air of calmness and knowledge. We went into the Explorer's Hall, which is open to the public. I can remember thinking, I visit this kind of place, but now I'm on the other side, I've been commissioned by the National Geographic. *It was a good moment. Then we went upstairs to see Kent Kobersteen, the Senior Assistant Editor for Photography. There was a meeting to finalise the planning, and to look at the contract. The whole thing took about two hours. And suddenly I was back outside, in the heat, with the traffic noise and the fumes. Only then did I get this heavy feeling of responsibility: now I had to deliver.'*

From that moment on, there was no doubt in Tomlinson's mind that this Whitbread would be different. The idea to involve the *National Geographic* had originally come from a US entry, *Clipper/Red Jacket*. They had approached the magazine, offering to take a writer and photographer on the boat for one leg. The *National Geographic* was enthusiastic and Angus Phillips, from the *Washington Post*, was appointed to write the article. Back in the spring of 1996, the magazine had asked for portfolio submissions from four photographers, of which Tomlinson was one.

Meanwhile, in Sweden, Johan Salén was preparing another Whitbread campaign. This time he had the language school company, EF, as a sponsor, with Magnus Olsson as his Sailing Director. They were preparing a two-boat entry, one with an all-male crew, the other with an all-female crew. Inevitably, after the success of *Intrum Justitia*, they wanted Tomlinson as the team's photographer. The fact that there were now two boats meant that it was impossible for him to cover all the sailing. And discussions started on the nature of his involvement. Tomlinson still hadn't heard from the *National Geographic* when he agreed to work with Team EF. But he was hopeful that if the magazine did commission his on-board photography for one leg, he could dovetail it with the Team EF job. This possibility was left open in the arrangement with EF. The remaining question was how much sailing Tomlinson would do with Team EF, and on which boats.

When the *National Geographic* contacted Tomlinson to say he had been selected as their photographer, the final pieces started to fall into place. By the early summer of 1997, time was running out for the *Clipper/Red Jacket* team, who were still unable to confirm their participation – and ultimately they didn't make the start line. Tomlinson put the *National Geographic* in touch with Salén, and they agreed that

EF Language *storms into the Southern Ocean on Leg 2.*

a Team EF boat would be the subject of the article. After that it was just a question of detail, which was sorted out in trans-Atlantic negotiation and on Tomlinson's visit to Washington. The original concept had been to take both writer and photographer on the boat. But with only twelve crew, this was never a particularly realistic proposition. It was decided that Tomlinson would race the whole leg, with Angus Phillips joining the boat from a fast motor launch for the last twenty-four hours. The rules allowed an extra, media-related person aboard for this period.

The *National Geographic's* needs now had to be integrated into Team EF's programme. Different options were discussed at a final meeting in Sweden with Tomlinson, Salén and both the skippers, Paul Cayard and Christine Guillou. The decision was made that Tomlinson would sail the first leg on the women's boat, and the second leg with the men. On both boats he would be part of the crew as well as photographer. It was the second leg, through the Southern Ocean from Cape Town to Fremantle (the first of the race's two Southern Ocean legs), that would form the basis of the *National Geographic* article. The reasoning behind the choice of legs was much the same as for the two legs Tomlinson did aboard *The Card*. The first leg was essential to fill the library with photos as soon as the race started. And they chose the first rather than the second Southern Ocean leg because of the long lead time for the *National Geographic*.

Next, Tomlinson approached the Swedish publisher, Max Strom, with the concept for a book. Behind Max Strom was Jeppe Wikstrom, the man who had distributed Tomlinson's Whitbread photographs in Sweden for the previous two races. They quickly agreed to publish what would become Risk to Gain - the story of Team EF's Whitbread Race. The pressure was inexorably building. Tomlinson's pictures would be analysed by the most respected photographic magazine in the world. And he had only two legs of sailing in which to fill 250 pages of book with colour photography. This race would provide a much bigger showcase than any that had gone before. And would require a wider variety of work than he had produced in the past. With this in mind, Tomlinson prepared very carefully indeed.

Unsurprisingly, the march of technology had provided substantial upgrades to the equipment. There was a permanent media station aboard the boat: a computer connected to the satellite communications system, dedicated to the sending of digital still and video footage. Digital cameras had removed the need to process film on board. For the first leg, as in 1993-94, Tomlinson packed two camera bodies and one waterproof compact, the 16 mm and 20 mm lenses, and the 80-200 mm telephoto lens, along with two flash guns. He put aboard a hundred rolls of film, and in addition there was a digital still camera for the transmission of images off the boat.

The first leg lasted thirty-five days, during which Tomlinson was confined to a sixty-foot boat with eleven women, with little contact with the outside world. Such a gender imbalance, for so long, in such confined quarters, was a rare experience. Afterwards, Tomlinson felt there was little difference to sailing with an all-male crew. The two teams had trained together, often mixed, for long periods of time. It was only because of the two skippers' different approaches that the atmosphere varied. Guillou was a less intense, more team-orientated leader than Cayard.

It was on the first leg that Tomlinson started to reopen his photographic horizons, to look beyond the staple angles and techniques he had established in the previous races. The need and the opportunity to fill all those magazine and book pages

Above and Right: EF Education *enjoys perfect Atlantic sailing on Leg 1.*

provided the imperative. One new technique that he experimented with on the first leg, and used to great effect in the second, was hand-held, night-time, long-exposure shots. Tomlinson would open the shutter for five seconds or so, in low light conditions, before using flash. The five seconds of hand-held exposure would provide the feeling of motion, while the flash created a stable enough image to give meaning to the movement.

On the second leg, he used the technique of standing at the shrouds during the Southern Ocean storms, in conditions when a tripod or clamp simply wouldn't have worked. The reward was dramatic new images, with a much greater sensation of speed than he had achieved before. For such exposure to the elements, Tomlinson had packed even more equipment for the second leg. He took four of the Nikon SLR camera bodies, with the normal lenses, plus a new 20-35 mm zoom lens. He also took a second waterproof compact, the two flash guns and another hundred rolls of film. He was only too aware that nothing must go wrong on the second leg. It was the biggest job of his life. Cayard was concerned to keep the weight down aboard the boat. And while the skipper also understood that Tomlinson had to get the job done, he was never told specifically what equipment Rick had packed on board the boat!

The sixteen days of that second leg were an intense experience, particularly as many of the crew were blooded in a Southern Ocean that only a handful had previously visited. But for Tomlinson there was no time to relax after the arrival in Fremantle. The entire package of unprocessed film was flown to Washington to be developed in the *National Geographic*'s own laboratories. The magazine had first and exclusive use on all the material from this leg, retained until ninety days after the National Geographic article was published. They could also use the images non-exclusively after that, with further payment. None of those images were seen in another publication until that period had elapsed. That wasn't too hard a limitation for Team EF to accept. Even added together, the circulation of all the sailing magazines in the world is unlikely to reach the *National Geographic*'s ten million copies, and its estimated four readers for each.

Tomlinson followed the film to Washington two days later. He worked with the picture editor right from the first selection to the final approval from the top editorial level. Unlike most magazines, where the photographer has nothing to do with the picture selection, the *National Geographic* involved him all the way through. With such a huge range of material covered by the magazine, they cannot be expert on everything. The person who took the pictures can often supply a great deal of useful knowledge. The magazine is very conscious of its status as a definitive reference publication. All the material underwent an extensive fact-checking process. Leg two ended for *EF Language* on November 25, 1997; the story went out in the May 1998 issue of the *National Geographic*.

As soon as the picture selection had final approval, Tomlinson was back on a plane to London. Then on to Fremantle – all within a week – where he was to shoot the restart. The men's boat, *EF Language*, went on to win the race. And from now on, it would be different for Tomlinson. The man who had practically invented on-board Whitbread photography had, he said, permanently joined the ranks in the helicopters and press boats. That was to be his last leg on a Whitbread racer. And the *National Geographic* article that is its record remains his proudest achievement.

EF Language, *a handheld shot with a five second shutter speed,*
using flash to provide sharpness within the motion.

Desperate action aboard EF Language.

Left: A spinnaker wrap at night.

Above: Retrieving the spinnaker sock.

Pushing the limit in the Southern Ocean.

Chapter 12
Crystal Ball Gazing

Hamble 2000 – Looking into the Future.

'I think that there are two main strands to my future as a photographer. The first is the question of how race-boat pictures are going to move forward from where they are now, and what part I can play in that. The second is a more personal desire to go and explore interesting places, looking for great images, whether it be of boats, ice, desert or wild animals.

'The answer to the first question is complex and unclear. Perhaps we should look back to look forward? Beken was first, with his magnificent yacht portraiture. Then came Alistair Black, who showed everyone that it could be more about action and people. He gave sailing photography a much more athletic perspective. I'm not sure that we've moved on from what Alistair showed us could be done. We might have got better at it, and the equipment has certainly got better, but it's essentially the same image that we're all still looking for – so where does it go next? I don't have the answer to that, but there are some possible avenues that may lead us forward.

'The fact that I was prepared to go to the Southern Ocean on the race boats, where the real action happens, has perhaps given me an edge over other photographers. I've now acknowledged that those days are almost over, the race is too competitive. Which leaves the question: how do I keep that edge? It's easy to end up as just another photographer in a chase boat with an 80-200 mm lens on one camera, and a 300 mm lens on the other. The most obvious answer is one that's been around for a long while, which is to shoot the deep ocean action from a photo chase boat. More particularly, to take a photo boat into the Southern Ocean, to record the Volvo Ocean Race. Conditions down there are amazing, and have provided me with so many memorable images – but there's not a single one from off the boat. The problem is that doing this would require quite massive resources. It needs a special type of boat, one that can cross oceans, and keep pace with a V.O. 60 averaging seventeen knots. They're not cheap to build or run.

'Along with Adrian Thompson, the designer of Pete Goss and Team Philips' catamaran, we looked at doing it with a VSV (Very Slender Vessel, or Wavepiercer) a few years back. There have been plenty of people who have talked about sending a ship around with the boats, with RIBs and helicopters aboard. The VSV is different, but it would still cost about the same as a whole Volvo Ocean Race campaign, and the money isn't available at the moment. Perhaps the first step is a big, powerful offshore RIB, that could follow the boats for the first and last twenty-four hours of the race. With nine legs, there are plenty of opportunities to follow starts and meet finishes. On the shorter legs it might be possible to follow them all the way. I suspect that my willingness to go offshore like this, and my ability to work in extreme conditions, is where I'll continue to find an edge in my photography. And perhaps it'll open some new directions in marine photography. I've built a ten-metre RIB with that in mind. Having a cabin will even allow us to send digital images back while offshore, using laptop computers and mobile or satellite phone links.

'For the inshore action, the future is less clear. There are now plenty of people working from RIBs and helicopters with the 80-200 mm and 300 mm lenses. And with good reason: boats look good through a telephoto lens, it compresses the action. One possibility is to shoot from higher off the water, in a RIB, from some kind of tuna tower. Wide angle doesn't look so good, because all the action seems to drop away from the viewer unless you can get really close. Perhaps that means being in the water with a fully waterproof camera at mark roundings. But then you only have thirty-six shots on a roll of film before you have to reload aboard a boat. It's not many. The same goes for something much smaller and nippier like a jetski; although it's very wet in a breeze, it would be a possible platform.

'Digital cameras may eventually come to our aid here. Some current memory cards can carry

A prototype Very Slender Vessel (VSV). Could this be a future platform for Southern Ocean photography?

about seventy images, twice as many as a roll of film. But their resolution is not good enough for high-quality reproduction yet. It's a real hassle at the moment, because we have to shoot with both film and digital. The same lenses fit the digital and film camera bodies, but you need to have both hanging around your neck. I can't wait for the time when digital resolutions match and surpass film. Then film will disappear, and with it the fifteen- to twenty-thousand-pound bill that I get every year for film and processing. In theory that goes straight on the bottom line. But I suspect I'll end up spending the money on the digital technology instead.

'The technology is also going to have a much wider impact on what we do in yachting photography. It's clear that the Internet, and the growth of news-based websites covering sports like sailing, will almost certainly increase the demand for digital images. These will need to be delivered very quickly, at relatively low resolutions. And there you find another influence on what we do: the end users of the image. For websites and news organisations, digital is already the answer. But if it's high-quality magazines and

calendars, then it has to be on film. I certainly think that whoever I shoot the next Volvo Ocean Race for, the vast majority of the material will be digital. The focus of the coverage has shifted to news – especially on the Internet, but even with the television. It's moved away from the traditional feature coverage by magazines and documentary-style television programmes. The media outlets will determine the technology we use, and perhaps influence the shooting style, the type of image as well.

'The other important influence on the way we photograph the sport is the way that sailing develops. One really noticeable change from a photographer's point of view is the shift to much lighter, high-tech boats. They don't move anywhere near as much water out of the way as they used to, and that makes it harder to get the action shot with spray everywhere. On the plus side, coloured Kevlar and PBO sails make much better pictures than white Dacron. The shift to a more professional sport, and the continuing influx of sponsorship money into sailing, are also going to have a positive impact.

'I think there's a general perception that all professional sports feed off personalities. People are going to become more important than boats. And perhaps the photography will start to focus on the individual much more than the race, as it does in football or golf. Perhaps this is the next step down the road that Alistair Black started us on. The problem for the photographer is all the hardware that surrounds the people on board. It needs to work for the shot, not against it. Perhaps we'll need to get much closer and use wide-angle lenses. Or we'll shift to 600 mm lenses. But that's a seriously difficult lens to shoot with from a small boat. Perhaps we need more stable platforms. But with courses being brought ever closer inshore, in the dinghies and match racing events in particular, then I suppose there's the possibility of shooting with a 600 mm from a tripod on the land, as they do in surfing and windsurfing. Then there's the potential for fixed cameras on the boat, with an off-the-boat operator who can control the camera remotely. Certainly, in events like the Volvo, the sailors are getting less and less interested in taking the pictures. This may be the only way we get images from on board in the future.

'It's also important to remember that this is still a business. I have to make a living out of it. We're always looking for new opportunities. One area is selling images as fine art prints. The French are leading

the way in this respect. There are photographers now who wait for storms and big seas, and then go out in helicopters and photograph them crashing into lighthouses and headlands. But they have many more relevant outlets in France. We've thought about opening a gallery for some time, but haven't managed to find the right location yet. However, the market is changing, the big marine booksellers are giving a lot more space to selling the poster images and prints that the consumer is demanding. Another similar opportunity is the interior decoration of office space. We recently completed a set of forty prints for Credit Suisse's new office in Canary Wharf. I can see this becoming another outlet for the high-quality image.

'It's difficult to sum it all up and get a clear view of where it's going, or where I'm going in particular. I think we can only say that the future is extremely exciting and definitely digital. But one thing will always remain true, whatever the image, whatever the technology, whatever the medium of transmission to the viewer: you only get the shot by being there. It doesn't come to me, and I certainly won't get it sitting in the office.'

Pete Goss' Open 50 and Yves Parlier's Open 60 – boats from the rule that has consistently pushed the technical development of long-distance ocean racing.

10/8/99

owers to record

Rock and roll: John Kostecki sets the pace as the German Illbruck team lead the Volvo 60s round the Rock

Top: Tomlinson arrived in a helicopter for a pre-planned photo shoot just as Team Philips *started to break-up. The pictures were wired to newspapers and websites all over the world.*

Above and Right: This image of the V.O. 60, illbruck, *was shot on a digital camera, and wired back from a RIB by the Fastnet Rock in time to make the daily newspapers.*

from everywhere. The trimmer's cockpit is worst. It's not covered by water — it's completely under it."

At these speeds, Peyron had only the leeward one of the boat's three hulls in the water. "Flying the boat is easy," he said nonchalantly. "Landing it is the hard part, because the sea was so confused.

" The rudders are vibrating hard in the turbulence. Sometimes they stall, the boat has sudden leeward helm and the tiller hits you in the chest," he added.

Peyron's highly experienced crew have great famil-

iarity with their boat, a 1990 creation from Britain's Nigel Irens, the main modification being the addition of a wing mast which cants to windward to generate extra lift. Even so, Peyron said he heard them muttering when the boat was being pushed. "that's a crazy guy on the tiller."

It took the next two 60ft multihulls a further 13 hours to reach the Rock, Francois Joyon's Banque *Populaire* leading Ellen MacArthur's *Kingfisher* round at 3.04am yesterday, with Ross Field's New Zealand Maxi One *Design* the first monohull,

some two and a half hours later, at 5.50am.

In the train of boats that followed, individual contests were played out class by class. American John Kostecki leading the German *Ill-bruck* team was the first Volvo 60 and 11th yacht round at 7.16am, a full hour ahead of Belgium's Volvo 60 *Yess,* with Grant Dalton and Adrian Stead aboard.

Leading the ILC-70 maxi was Jim Dolan's *Sagamore,* 12th at the Rock, and two minutes ahead of George Coumantaros' *Boomerang,* with Alberto Roemmers' *Alexia* 12 minutes later and

Larry Ellison and Ted Turner's *Sayonara* a further 21 minutes further back.

Slotting in between ILC-70s were the Open 60 monohulls, with Catherine Chabaud's *Whirlpool* a full 2hr 11min ahead of Mike Golding's *Team Group 4.* This is Golding's first outing since pulling out of last winter's Around Alone race.

Behind the serious racing tackle, Charles Dunstone's Swan 80 *Nokia Hamilton* was the first mainstream competitor round at 2.25pm and four roundings after her, in 25th place, came Peter Harrison's Farr 50 *Chernikeeff.*

Unusual angles:

Above: Used up close and on-board, the wide-angle lens gives an interesting and surreal feel to this image of the Open 60 Gartmore.

Below: Fleet action through a wide-angle lens.

These Pages and Overleaf: Pete Goss has used the
Very Slender Vessel (VSV) *principles in his*
Team Phillips *catamaran, built for The Race.*